BIBLE ADVENTURE

DEVOTIONS

for Kids

PAUL KENT

for Kids

BARBOUR **kidz**
A Division of Barbour Publishing

Published by Barbour Publishing, Inc., 1810 Barbour Drive, Uhrichsville, Ohio 44683, www.barbourbooks.com

Our mission is to inspire the world with the life-changing message of the Bible.

Printed in the United States of America.

001593   0423   BP

WELCOME TO

BIBLE ADVENTURE DEVOTIONS FOR KIDS!

Some say the Christian life is an adventure. What does that mean?

Well, think of adventure movies: There's a lot of action with some quiet times in between. There are highs and lows, smiles and tears, victories and defeats. There's a big goal that seems impossible to reach. And there's usually a happy ending.

In our Christian lives, God sends times of action and rest. We'll face good and bad, happy and sad as we pursue the faraway goal of heaven. But for everyone who really follows Jesus—everyone who chooses the adventure of faith—there's an incredible ending.

Dozens of Bible characters chose the adventure of knowing, loving, and serving God. In this book, you'll meet many of them—Moses, Paul, Deborah, Daniel, three different Marys, a couple of Johns, and some less familiar people like Gaius and Benaiah.

Each one's adventure was unique. Some fought enemy armies. Some visited new places and learned new things. Some were totally about helping others. All of them are examples for us today.

So whether you'd rather explore a steaming volcano or knit mittens for needy kids, you'll find a friend or two in the pages that follow. Read on for adventure!

MOSES:
THE BIGGEST ADVENTURE

Whenever Moses went into the meeting tent, the cloud would come down and stand at the door of the tent. And the Lord would speak with Moses. . . . The Lord spoke to Moses face to face, as a man speaks to his friend.

EXODUS 33:9, 11

As the handpicked leader of God's special people, Moses was surrounded by miracles. First, God called out to him from a flaming bush that never burned up. When Moses threw his staff—his walking stick—to the ground, it turned into a live snake. Moses called down ten terrible plagues to make the Egyptian Pharaoh free the Israelites from their awful slavery. The waters of the Red Sea split in two when Moses raised his arm, and the people walked through on perfectly dry ground. And when God gave the Ten Commandments to Moses, Mount Sinai rumbled with thunder, flashed with lightning, and shook with an earthquake.

But none of these amazing events was the biggest adventure of Moses' life. The most important and exciting thing he ever did was *talk with God*. Moses wasn't perfect, but he loved and followed God. They spent happy times together, like friends do.

And you can do exactly the same thing. How? By reading God's Word. By talking to Him in prayer and then quietly listening for His reply. He will "speak" to you through your thoughts, in words that agree with His words in the Bible.

When you do these things, you step into the biggest adventure of your life.

Nothing can compare to knowing the one true God, the Creator and keeper of the entire universe. And not just knowing *about* Him—you can actually *know God* like you know your best friend here on earth. Take a tip from Moses: your adventure starts with talking to God.

BIBLE ADVENTURE PRAYER STARTER

Father in heaven, I want to talk with You like I talk to my best friend. Help me to read and understand Your Word, the Bible. And give me the "spiritual ears" to listen for Your voice when I pray. I look forward to this adventure with You!

BIBLE ADVENTURE MEMORY VERSE

The Lord is near to all who call on Him, to all who call on Him in truth.
PSALM 145:18

JESUS:
ULTIMATE MISSIONARY

Jesus said to the followers, "Let us go to the towns near here so I can preach there also. That is why I came." He went through Galilee. He preached in their places of worship and put out demons.
MARK 1:38–39

~~~~~~~~~~~~~~~~

Think for a minute about the word *missionary*. A missionary is a person on a mission—to tell other people about Jesus. Some missionaries travel around the world to preach about salvation. Jesus Himself traveled from heaven to earth to share the good news!

The fact that there's good news means there is also bad news. The bad news is that all people—every one of us—have sinned. We choose to do wrong, and we can't please God. We all deserve to be punished. On our own, nobody can come to God and become part of His family. But Jesus said in the scripture above, "That is why I came."

You've probably heard Jesus called the "Son of God," and that's exactly who He is. But Jesus is also *God*. It's hard for us to understand, but our God is one God in three persons—God the Father, Jesus the Son, and the Holy Spirit. Our three-in-one God is called the "Trinity."

Going back in time forever, Jesus had lived happily with the Father and the Spirit. But at just the right time, Jesus left the perfection of heaven to come live on this messed-up earth. He became the ultimate missionary! Jesus walked along the dusty roads of Galilee and Judea to tell people how to be saved by believing that He is "the Way and the Truth and the Life" (John 14:6).

When you receive Jesus as your Lord and Savior, you start the adventure of a lifetime—an adventure for all eternity. The ultimate missionary is calling you to follow Him today. Will you do it?

BIBLE ADVENTURE PRAYER STARTER

Lord Jesus, thank You for coming from heaven to earth to show me how to be saved. I want to be part of God's family by believing in You!

BIBLE ADVENTURE MEMORY VERSE

"There is no way to be saved from the punishment of sin through anyone else. For there is no other name under heaven given to men by which we can be saved."
ACTS 4:12

MARY, MOTHER OF JESUS:
GIRLS HAVE ADVENTURES TOO!

The angel said to her, "Mary, do not be afraid.
You have found favor with God. See! You are
to become a mother and have a Son. You are
to give Him the name Jesus. He will be great.
He will be called the Son of the Most High."

LUKE 1:30-32

~~~~~~~~~~~

Adventures aren't just for those guys who fight giants or survive fiery furnaces. Who ever had an experience like Mary did?

She was young—maybe only a few years older than you—when an angel suddenly visited her. That must have been amazing all by itself. But then Gabriel, who had come directly from God's presence, shared some mind-blowing news with Mary. She was going to give birth to God's Son, Jesus.

Talk about an adventure! The Jewish people had been waiting for God's Messiah for hundreds of years. Many girls had dreamed of becoming the mother of the Savior. And now Mary knew that *she* was the one.

Since she wasn't married yet, Mary asked Gabriel how she could become pregnant with Jesus. The angel told her that God's Spirit would take care of that. And Mary humbly said, "I am willing to be used of the Lord. Let it happen to me as you have said" (Luke 1:38).

Mary's life changed forever. In a few months, she would give birth to Jesus. Over the following years, she watched Him grow up through boyhood, preach and teach and perform miracles, and then die on the cross for the sins of the world. That was incredibly hard for her. But soon she saw Jesus alive again! Mary knew that she—and anyone else who believes in Jesus—would receive eternal life.

Mary accepted God's plan for her life, and that plan truly changed the world. Don't you think that's even more exciting than defeating a giant?

BIBLE ADVENTURE PRAYER STARTER

Heavenly Father, I want to do my part to help others know You through Jesus. Please use me in the big adventure of growing Your kingdom.

BIBLE ADVENTURE MEMORY VERSE

*"Our Father in heaven, Your name
is holy. May Your holy nation come.
What You want done, may it be done
on earth as it is in heaven."*
MATTHEW 6:9–10

DAVID:
SPEAKING OF GIANTS. . .

David said, "The Lord Who saved me from the foot of the lion and from the foot of the bear, will save me from the hand of this Philistine."
1 SAMUEL 17:37

~~~~~~~~~~

The story of Mary giving birth to Jesus is amazing. But David's fight with Goliath is pretty cool too.

You probably know much of the story: David was the youngest of eight boys, the sons of Jesse. His three oldest brothers were soldiers in Israel's army led by King Saul. They were camped in the Valley of Elah, across from the Philistines. And the enemy had a not-so-secret weapon called Goliath—a monstrous warrior over nine feet tall!

Goliath was as mean as he was big. Day after day, he would shout insults at Saul's soldiers. He challenged them to a one-on-one fight. Of course no one on Israel's side wanted to do *that*. And then David entered the picture.

The kid brother was watching sheep back home when Jesse gave him a job: to take some food to his soldier brothers. When David arrived at the camp, he saw Goliath challenging Israel's soldiers. Since nobody else was willing to fight, David volunteered—and you definitely know what happened next. With a single shot from his sling, the shepherd kid knocked down the huge, tough warrior. Then David used Goliath's own sword to cut off his head.

How could David be so adventurous and brave? Because he knew the one true God, who was so much bigger and stronger than Goliath.

King Saul couldn't imagine David defeating such a powerful enemy. But David said he had already killed a lion and a bear with nothing but his hands. God protected David then and would see him through this fight with Goliath. That's exactly what happened.

God will help us too. Our "giants" might be sickness or loneliness or fear. Maybe our parents' divorce or Grandma's car crash. Or maybe some other tough, scary thing. Just remember that God is always with you, and He's always on your side. No giant can stand against Him.

BIBLE ADVENTURE PRAYER STARTER

Mighty God, nothing compares to You. Remind me of Your amazing strength so I don't need to be afraid of anything.

BIBLE ADVENTURE MEMORY VERSE

With Your help I can go against many soldiers. With my God I can jump over a wall.
PSALM 18:29

PAUL:
THE BIBLE WRITER

All the Holy Writings are God-given and are made alive by Him. Man is helped when he is taught God's Word. It shows what is wrong. It changes the way of a man's life. It shows him how to be right with God.

2 TIMOTHY 3:16

~~~~~~

Ever wonder where the Bible came from? That's a great question!

The short answer is *God*. We call the Bible "God's Word" because it tells us what He said about Himself and us, sin and salvation, and many other important things.

The longer answer is that God used about forty people over sixteen centuries to put His words on paper. Men like Moses, David, Solomon, Matthew, and Peter all wrote parts of the Bible. And then there was Paul.

As a young man, he was known as Saul—and he *hated* Jesus. He caused trouble for Christians, even hoping to get them killed. But one day Jesus shined a bright light from heaven on Saul, blinding him for a few days. A voice asked Saul why he wanted to hurt Jesus. And Saul learned that he had a new job—not hurting Christians, but becoming one himself. He would no longer try to stop the message of Jesus but share it everywhere he went. Talk about a miraculous change!

In another change, Saul was soon called Paul, and part of his new job was writing down God's Word. God would "inspire" Paul with important truths. Then Paul would write those truths in his own words. Of the twenty-seven New Testament books, he wrote thirteen—including Romans, Galatians, Philippians, and two letters to Timothy.

As Paul told Timothy in the verse above, the Bible has the life of God in it. When we read the Bible—and do what it says—we become right with God. Nothing is more important than that.

It's amazing to think that God used a guy like Paul to write so much of the Bible. The Jesus hater became one of Jesus' closest followers, then left us words that can truly change our lives. Let's be sure we read and obey them!

BIBLE ADVENTURE PRAYER STARTER

Lord, I thank You for Your Word. Give me the desire to know it and the courage to obey it.

BIBLE ADVENTURE MEMORY VERSE

*Your Word is a lamp to my feet
and a light to my path.*
PSALM 119:105

NOAH:
STANDING ALONE

This is the story of Noah and his family. Noah was right with God. He was without blame in his time. Noah walked with God. . . . Now the earth was sinful in the eyes of God. The earth was filled with people hurting each other.

GENESIS 6:9, 11

~~~~~~~~~~~~~~~~

Be yourself! Do your own thing! Don't let anyone tell you what to do!

In this world, you'll hear a lot of that. And there is *some* truth in it. You should be yourself and do your own thing—but only in the ways God wants. And never let anyone tell you what to do if their words go against God's Word.

You see, God sets the rules. Because He made this world and keeps it going, He has every right to say what people should and shouldn't do. Sadly, many people want to fight against God. They do that now, and they did it thousands of years ago, in the days when Noah lived.

Everyone has heard of Noah and his ark full of animals. What makes the story so amazing is that Noah and his family were *the only good people on earth*. God was so angry at sin and violence that He decided to wipe out everyone else with a huge flood. Noah was the RESET button.

Why would Noah be the one to reset the whole human race? Because he was "right with God" and "without blame in his time." Noah followed God's rules in God's way. He didn't let the rest of the world drag him down into sin. He didn't cheat or lie or steal or hurt people the way everyone else did.

In other words, Noah was truly himself—as God called him to be. He did his own thing, which was really God's thing. He didn't let anyone tell him to do wrong—he listened only to God. Noah stood alone, and God did great things for him and through him.

You can be like Noah too. Stand alone against this world, and God will take care of the rest.

BIBLE ADVENTURE PRAYER STARTER

Lord, I want to stand alone against this world. But I'll never really be alone because You'll always be with me!

BIBLE ADVENTURE MEMORY VERSE

"Do not follow many people in doing wrong."
Exodus 23:2

JOHN THE BAPTIST:
THE GOAT

Jesus began to tell the people about John the Baptist. He said, "Why did you go out to the desert? Did you go out to see a small tree moving in the wind? What did you go out to see? A man dressed in good clothes? Those who are dressed in good clothes are in the houses of kings. But what did you go to see? One who speaks for God? Yes, I tell you, he is more than one who speaks for God. . . . I tell you, of those born of women, there is no one greater than John the Baptist."
LUKE 7:24–26, 28

~~~~~~~~~~~

Have you ever seen some athlete called the "GOAT"? That's an acronym—a word made from the first letters of several words—meaning "**G**reatest **O**f **A**ll **T**ime." According to Jesus, John the Baptist was the GOAT—of all people everywhere.

What made John so great? He was a relative of Jesus, and God sent him ahead to "make the way ready for the Lord" (Matthew 3:3). He preached repentance, telling people to turn toward Jesus, "the Lamb of God Who takes away the sin of the world!" (John 1:29). John lived and died in total obedience to God, always pointing others to Jesus. No wonder Jesus thought John was special.

But Jesus said something else in Luke 7:28. Here's the last part of that verse: "The least in the holy nation of God is greater than he." If you follow Jesus, God thinks *you're* greater than the greatest!

Sometimes we feel unimportant. Maybe we're not as smart or as good looking or as talented as someone else. It's easy to feel sorry for ourselves. But when we do that, we're not living our faith adventure the way we should. If you're ever feeling sad or lonely, go straight to God. Tell Him how you feel and ask for His help. He thinks you're pretty special, you know.

BIBLE ADVENTURE PRAYER STARTER

Heavenly Father, thank You for loving me. It's so nice to know that because I believe in Jesus, You think I'm great!

BIBLE ADVENTURE MEMORY VERSE

I know that nothing can keep us from the love of God. Death cannot! Life cannot! Angels cannot! Leaders cannot! Any other power cannot! Hard things now or in the future cannot!
ROMANS 8:38

MARY MAGDALENE:
FRIEND OF JESUS

*It was the first day of the week.
Mary Magdalene came to the grave
early in the morning while it was
still dark. She saw that the stone had
been pushed away from the grave.*
JOHN 20:1

~~~~~~~~~

Jesus' enemies called Him a "friend of sinners." They wanted to embarrass Him. But since everybody is a sinner and everyone needs a friend, that "insult" was actually a compliment.

Mary Magdalene was one of Jesus' closest friends. His "twelve disciples" were all guys, but Jesus had female followers too. He had cast seven demons from Mary. How incredible to be set free from that terrible problem! Mary became one of Jesus' most loyal followers. Wherever He went, Mary Magdalene tagged along. She must have been wealthy, because she and a few other women helped pay the way for Jesus and His disciples.

When Jesus was arrested and put on trial, all the guys who followed Him ran away. But not Mary Magdalene. She and some other women saw Jesus raised up on the cross. They watched a strange midday darkness fall over the land. They felt the earth shake when Jesus died. They saw where two brave men—Nicodemus and Joseph—put Jesus' body in a cave-like tomb.

That all happened on a Friday. The next day, the Sabbath, nobody was allowed to work. But early on Sunday, Mary and the other women rushed to Jesus' tomb. They wanted to put spices on His body because dead people soon begin to stink.

But Jesus wasn't dead—He'd come back to life! And the very first person He met was His dear friend Mary. Her tears of sadness quickly became tears of joy.

Jesus is a friend to everyone who follows Him. But He wants us to do more than just follow—He wants us to really, truly *love* Him. Let's be like Mary Magdalene and spend as much time as we can with Jesus. Let's listen to Him—we'll "hear" Him when we read the Bible. Let's honor and serve and give to Jesus. When we do, we'll enjoy the most perfect friendship ever.

BIBLE ADVENTURE PRAYER STARTER

Lord Jesus, thank You for being my friend. I want to be the best friend I can be to You!

BIBLE ADVENTURE MEMORY VERSE

"No one can have greater love than to give his life for his friends."
JOHN 15:13

ELISHA:
MIRACLE MAN

When the Syrians came against him, Elisha prayed to the Lord, saying, "Make these people blind, I pray." So the Lord made them blind.
2 KINGS 6:18

~~~~~~~~~~~~~~

If you were asked to explain what miracles are, could you? Here's one way: miracles are unusual—even impossible—events beyond human power or understanding. If they're beyond what people can do, they must come from God.

The Bible is full of miracles, like the Red Sea splitting in two for the Israelites to cross. Or the walls of Jericho falling as Joshua's army shouted. Or Jesus healing diseases, walking on water, and turning one small lunch into enough food for five thousand people. All of these unusual events were powered by God, who can do anything He pleases.

For some reason, the Lord liked to do miracles through the prophet Elisha. This man cured an enemy army commander of leprosy. He made an iron ax-head, which had fallen into the Jordan River, float up to the surface. He purified a poisoned stew for some other prophets. He blinded an enemy army, as you read in today's scripture. And he told an older woman who'd never had children that she would soon become pregnant with a son. Then years later, when the boy died suddenly, Elisha brought him back to life.

Elisha even performed a miracle after he was dead! According to 2 Kings 13:20–21, "Elisha died, and they buried him. Now groups of Moabite soldiers would come and fight in the land in the spring of the year. As a man was being buried, some Moabite soldiers were seen, so the man was thrown into Elisha's grave. When the man touched the bones of Elisha, he came alive and stood up on his feet."

Remember, miracles are powered by God—He just uses people like Elisha to perform them. If God created the whole universe just by speaking (and He did), then He can do things that seem crazy and impossible to us. Miracles aren't hard at all for God—and He still does them today.

Keep your eyes open to what God is doing in your world. You might be surprised at what you see!

BIBLE ADVENTURE PRAYER STARTER

Lord, show me Your power by the amazing things You do every day!

BIBLE ADVENTURE MEMORY VERSE

Great is our Lord, and great in power.
PSALM 147:5

LUKE:
RENAISSANCE MAN

Luke, the dear doctor, and Demas say hello.
COLOSSIANS 4:14

~~~~~~~~~~~~~~~~~

Ever heard of a "Renaissance man"? Luke was a Renaissance man long before anyone had even heard the word.

The Renaissance (pronounced *REN-uh-sontz*) was a period of time, about four hundred to seven hundred years ago. In Europe, artists, writers, and scientists were coming on strong. People like Leonardo da Vinci—he painted the famous *Mona Lisa*—drew up plans for unheard-of things like adding machines and aircraft and wrote all about them in his journals. So a Renaissance man (or woman) is someone familiar with, and good at, a lot of things.

The Bible says Luke was a doctor (Colossians 4:14), and some old traditions even claim that he was a painter. He was a careful historian who wrote a big part of the New Testament: the Gospel of Luke and the book of Acts. Clearly, Luke was smart and talented—and he used his abilities to help spread the good news about Jesus.

Luke traveled with the apostle Paul, which was always an adventure. People who hated Paul's message often stirred up trouble for him. The opposition got so bad that Paul was forced to sail to Rome for a trial before the emperor, Caesar. On the way, a wild, two-week storm destroyed the ship. But Paul, Luke, and all of the other 274 people on board were miraculously saved (Acts 27:37). Toward the end of Paul's life, when he was expecting to be put to death, he wrote, "Luke is the only one with me here" (2 Timothy 4:11).

Some people, like Luke, are smart and brave and able to do all kinds of good things. We might look at them and say, "Of course God will use *them*!" But God has a job for each one of us, whether we're a Renaissance kid or just an average, everyday guy or girl.

The good things you enjoy and do well are God's "gifts" to you. Ask Him what your gifts are, and then use them to help others and point them to Jesus!

BIBLE ADVENTURE PRAYER STARTER

Heavenly Father, please help me to know what my gifts are. Then show me how to use them to help others. I want people to know Jesus!

BIBLE ADVENTURE MEMORY VERSE

We all have different gifts that God has given to us by His loving-favor. We are to use them.
ROMANS 12:6

JOSHUA:
GOD'S STRANGE WAYS

*Now the gates of Jericho were all shut
because of the people of Israel. No one went
out and no one came in. The Lord said to
Joshua, "See, I have given Jericho into
your hand, with its king and soldiers."*

JOSHUA 6:1–2

~~~~~~~~~~~~~~~

Joshua was a man of war. The first time he appears in the Bible, he'd been ordered by Moses to lead an army against the Amalekites. Joshua obeyed and "destroyed Amalek and his people with the sword" (Exodus 17:13).

That was during Israel's escape from slavery in Egypt, an event called the "Exodus." (Now you know why the second book of the Bible has its name!) As the Israelites came close to their promised land, Moses gave Joshua another military job. He would be one of twelve soldiers sent into Canaan to spy out the land.

This guy was tough and knew how to fight. But when it was time to lead the people into Canaan, Joshua got some very strange orders from God.

The Israelites needed to defeat Jericho, an enemy city surrounded by tall, thick walls. But they wouldn't use ladders or ropes, catapults or battering rams. They would walk, blow trumpets, and shout.

Really, God?

Yes, really. "Walk around the city," God told Joshua. "Have all the men of war go around the city once. Do this for six days. . . . Then on the seventh day you will walk around the city seven times. And the religious leaders will blow horns. When you hear the long sound of the ram's horn, all the people should call out with a loud noise. The wall of the city will fall to the ground" (Joshua 6:3–5).

Joshua followed God's orders exactly, and God did exactly what He promised. The walls of Jericho fell flat. Then the Israelites rushed in to destroy everyone inside.

Sometimes God's ways are much different than ours. But His ways are always the best! If the Bible's rules seem strange or hard, obey them anyway. You'll find, as Joshua did, that God knows what He's doing.

BIBLE ADVENTURE PRAYER STARTER

Lord God, I may not always understand Your ways—but I trust that You know best. Give me the courage to obey.

BIBLE ADVENTURE MEMORY VERSE

"For My thoughts are not your thoughts, and My ways are not your ways," says the Lord.
ISAIAH 55:8

ELIJAH:
A HUGE VICTORY. . .

Elijah the man who spoke for God came near and said, "O Lord, God of Abraham, Isaac and Israel, let it be known today that You are God in Israel. . . ." Then the fire of the Lord fell. It burned up the burnt gift, the wood, the stones and the dust. And it picked up the water that was in the ditch. All the people fell on their faces when they saw it. They said, "The Lord, He is God."
1 KINGS 18:36, 38–39

Imagine the scene: 450 prophets of the false god Baal stand against Elijah, prophet of the one true God. They are surrounded by an even larger crowd of watchers. Like a festival on the Fourth of July, it will end with fireworks. But this is no celebration.

Elijah shouts to the crowd, "How long will you be divided between two ways of thinking? If the Lord is God, follow Him. But if Baal is God, then follow him" (1 Kings 18:21).

The people say nothing, so Elijah sets up a contest. Baal's followers should build an altar, put firewood on it, and place the meat of a bull on top for a sacrifice. Elijah will do the same thing. Then each side will call on their god to send fire to their altar. Everyone agrees.

Baal's prophets pray and shout and dance, but no fire falls. So they get wilder, cutting themselves with swords. Still they receive no answer from their "god."

Elijah knows Baal is fake. Now he's going to prove it to everyone. But before he asks God to send fire, he calls for twelve big water jars. They're poured all over the altar. That's no way to make something burn.

But it's also no problem for the one true God. Elijah prays, and God sends a blast of fire that burns the soggy wood and meat. God's fire even destroys the rocks of the altar!

Now the people know which God is real. Hint: He's the same God who makes you part of His family through faith in Jesus.

BIBLE ADVENTURE PRAYER STARTER

Wow, God, You are amazing.
Thank You for Your power—but also
for Your love. I'm glad You're my Father!

BIBLE ADVENTURE MEMORY VERSE

You are the God Who does great works.
You have shown Your power among the people.
PSALM 77:14

ESTHER:
WHEN ADVENTURES TURN SCARY, PART 1

Mordecai answered, "Do not think that you in the king's special house will live any more than all the other Jews. For if you keep quiet at this time, help will come to the Jews from another place. But you and your father's house will be destroyed. Who knows if you have not become queen for such a time as this?"

ESTHER 4:13–14

~~~~~~~

Esther's story sounds like a reality game show. The king wants a new queen. Thousands of girls go through beauty treatments and training to try to win the contest. One sweet, beautiful young woman rises to the top, earning the king's thumbs-up. Hello, Queen Esther!

But this real-life, long-ago event wasn't all fun and games.

King Ahasuerus needed a new wife because he'd angrily kicked out Queen Vashti. The king's top official, Haman, was a mean, selfish guy who was willing to *kill* his political enemies. Esther wasn't sure what people would think about her Jewish nationality, so she kept it quiet. And even though she was queen, she could only see the king when he called for her. If Esther showed up when he was in a bad mood, she could be killed.

Then things got even worse.

One day her cousin Mordecai made Haman, a noble in the king's court, mad. Esther was an orphan—her parents were both gone. Mordecai had raised Esther like he was her dad. "Mr. Important" Haman thought everyone should bow down when he went by, but Mordecai, as one of God's people, refused. When Haman learned Mordecai was Jewish, he wanted to kill every Jew in Persia!

Now the pressure was on Esther. Should she go to the king? He could help protect her people. But if he was grouchy, she could be killed. Mordecai sent a message to his cousin, the words of Esther 4:13–14 above. The queen quietly asked her people to fast and pray for three days. Then she would risk her life for the Jews by going straight to the king.

What happened to Esther? Keep reading. . . .

BIBLE ADVENTURE PRAYER STARTER

Heavenly Father, there are scary things in this world. Please give me courage to face them, and protect me!

BIBLE ADVENTURE MEMORY VERSE

The world and all its desires will pass away. But the man who obeys God and does what He wants done will live forever.
1 JOHN 2:17

ESTHER:
WHEN ADVENTURES TURN SCARY, PART 2

When the king saw Esther the queen standing in the open space, she found favor in his eyes. . . . Then the king said to her, "What do you want, Queen Esther? What do you ask of me? You would be given even as much as half the nation."

ESTHER 5:2–3

Whew. . .when Esther went to King Ahasuerus, he was happy to see her. She risked her life for her people and survived—at least for now.

God had made Esther queen of Persia, a huge empire stretching from Africa to India. But even as queen, she faced danger. The king's top official, Haman, hated the Jews. Esther was Jewish. She'd spoken to the king and lived. Now she had to convince him to protect her people.

Esther was more than good looking—she was smart. When Ahasuerus asked what she wanted, she didn't mention Haman's evil plan. She just invited the king to dinner, along with Haman.

That night, both men enjoyed their meal. The king again asked Esther what she wanted. She still held back, simply inviting the two men to *another* dinner the next day.

Haman was proud. He'd been invited to two

straight meals with the king and queen. But as he bragged to his family, he remembered how angry he was with Mordecai. So Haman sent men to build a tower for a hanging.

When Haman and Ahasuerus attended the queen's second dinner, the king again said, "What do you want to ask of me?" Esther finally answered, "I ask that my life and the lives of my people be saved. . . . This sinful Haman hates us very much!" (Esther 7:2–3, 6).

Ahasuerus suddenly realized the truth: Esther was a good person; Haman was not. And the king ordered Haman hanged on his own tower.

Though it was scary and dangerous, Esther stood up for others. God calls Christians to do the same. Like Esther, we might win. But even if the very worst thing happens—we die—we'll end up in heaven. God will take care of us either way.

BIBLE ADVENTURE PRAYER STARTER

Lord, give me courage to stand up
for others. I want to be like Esther!

BIBLE ADVENTURE MEMORY VERSE

The angel of the Lord stays close
around those who fear Him, and
He takes them out of trouble.
PSALM 34:7

PETER:
TRAILBLAZER

*Peter said to Jesus, "If it is You, Lord,
tell me to come to You on the water."
Jesus said, "Come!" Peter got out of the
boat and walked on the water to Jesus.*
MATTHEW 14:28-29

~~~~~~~~~~~~~~~~~~~~~~~~~~~

Some people are trailblazers. They go places and do things that no one else has. Like Peter, one night on the Sea of Galilee.

Though it's called a "sea," this body of water is really a big lake. Storms can blow up quickly, and the water gets rough. Remember the time Jesus and His followers were in a boat in such a bad storm that the disciples thought they were going to die? The men had to wake Jesus from a nap, and He told the wind and waves to calm down—which they did.

Another time the disciples were in a boat without Jesus. The wind was getting stronger, and waves were tossing them around. Suddenly the guys saw something so weird they thought it was a ghost: Jesus was walking toward them on top of the water!

He called out, "Take hope. It is I. Do not be afraid!" (Matthew 14:27). And then Peter, who often spoke and acted before he thought, called back, "If it is You, Lord, tell me to come to You on the water." Jesus agreed, so Peter climbed down from the boat to do something no one besides Jesus has ever done: he walked on water too.

If the story stopped there, we'd say Peter is an amazing example to us: Follow Jesus anywhere! Never be afraid! Perform miracles! Except that Peter soon noticed the crazy wind. And the second he lost focus on Jesus—*splash!* He sank.

Happily for Peter, Jesus was right there to grab his hand and pull him back up. "You have so little faith!" Jesus said. "Why did you doubt?" (Matthew 14:31). They climbed into the boat, and the wind immediately calmed.

What can we learn from this? We can do amazing things with Jesus. But without Him, we're in trouble.

BIBLE ADVENTURE PRAYER STARTER

Lord Jesus, You are amazing. I want
to focus my whole life on You.

BIBLE ADVENTURE MEMORY VERSE

*"I am the Vine and you are the branches.
Get your life from Me. Then I will live
in you and you will give much fruit.
You can do nothing without Me."*
JOHN 15:5

MATTHIAS:
BECOMING A LEADER

They brought two men in front of them.
They were Joseph, also called Barsabbas
Justus, and Matthias. Then the followers
prayed, saying, "Lord, You know the hearts
of all men. Show us which of these two men
You have chosen. He is to take the place of
Judas in this work and be a missionary.
Judas lost his place and went where he
belonged because of sin." Then they drew
names and the name of Matthias was chosen.
ACTS 1:23–26

If you've spent any time in Sunday school or children's church, you've probably heard of the twelve disciples. Jesus chose them to follow Him, learning from Him as He taught and helped people. At some point, those men—including Peter, John, James, and Matthew—became the twelve *apostles*, no longer learners but teachers, missionaries sent out to tell others about Jesus.

You may also know that one of Jesus' followers was Judas Iscariot. For thirty silver coins, he betrayed Jesus to His enemies. Jesus was killed on a cross, and Judas felt so bad about what he'd done that he ran away and killed himself.

The other eleven apostles thought they needed

to replace Judas. So they looked around at Jesus' other disciples—He had a lot more than just twelve people who followed Him—and picked two good men who had been around since the beginning. They drew names, and Matthias became the new twelfth apostle.

Suddenly this good, faithful, hard worker was a leader in the church. What he had heard and seen and learned would be used to help other people know Jesus.

God is always developing new leaders for His church. Maybe someday *you'll* be one of them! For now, be like Matthias: good, faithful, and hard-working.

BIBLE ADVENTURE PRAYER STARTER

Lord Jesus, I want to be like Matthias— someone whose hard work and true faith leads to important jobs in Your church. Please help me to watch and listen and learn all I can.

BIBLE ADVENTURE MEMORY VERSE

Let no one show little respect for you because you are young. Show other Christians how to live by your life. They should be able to follow you in the way you talk and in what you do.
1 TIMOTHY 4:12

JONAH:
A SILLY ADVENTURE

The Word of the Lord came to Jonah the son of Amittai, saying, "Get up and go to the large city of Nineveh, and preach against it. For their sin has come up before Me." But Jonah ran away from the Lord going toward Tarshish. He went down to Joppa and found a ship which was going to Tarshish. Jonah paid money, and got on the ship to go with them, to get away from the Lord.
JONAH 1:1–3

The word *silly* can describe something funny. Sometimes it means "kind of dumb."

Everyone knows Jonah got swallowed by a giant fish. Fewer people know why he got into that strange spot: Jonah was trying to run away from God.

Yep. God sent the supersized fish to teach Jonah a lesson. This "adventure" was a silly one because Jonah never should have gone through it!

He was a prophet. That means God told him things to say, and then Jonah shared those words with others. One day God told Jonah to warn a certain city that it was going to be punished. Sinful Nineveh was the capital of Assyria, a mean, powerful enemy of Israel. Jonah thought, *No way*. So he jumped on a ship heading the opposite direction.

But the God who created the universe and keeps it running every day can't be fooled. He knew exactly where Jonah was. And God sent both the big fish and a big storm to turn His runaway prophet around. Jonah went over the side of the ship, straight into the fish's mouth. Then, for the three weirdest days ever, he thought things over. (What else was he going to do there?) Finally, he prayed, "I will give You what I have promised" (Jonah 2:9). Soon the fish spit Jonah out on shore.

Jonah went to Nineveh, and the people actually listened to him. They turned away from their sins. Had Jonah obeyed right away, he would have saved himself a lot of trouble and fear.

Let's not have any "silly adventures" of our own. When God says something, just do it!

BIBLE ADVENTURE PRAYER STARTER

Heavenly Father, make me wise. I don't ever want to have silly adventures because of my disobedience!

BIBLE ADVENTURE MEMORY VERSE

The fear of the Lord is the beginning of wisdom. All who obey His Laws have good understanding.
PSALM 111:10

RUTH:
RAGS TO RICHES

Boaz took Ruth. She became his wife, and he went in to her. The Lord made it possible for her to have a child and she gave birth to a son. The women said to Naomi, "Thanks be to the Lord. He has not left you without a family this day."

RUTH 4:13–14

~~~~~~~~~~~

Have you heard of a "rags-to-riches" story? *Cinderella* is one. And there are lots of them in pro sports. When someone starts out poor then suddenly becomes wealthy—by marrying a prince or getting a giant contract—we say they went from rags to riches.

In the Bible, Ruth was a poor widow who married a wealthy man. But she also became the great-grandmother of King David and an ancestor of Jesus. That's worth more than *tons* of gold!

Ruth was from the land of Moab. She married a Jewish man when he and his family moved to her country. They were escaping a famine—a food shortage—around Bethlehem.

Before long, Ruth's husband died. So did her father-in-law. Ruth loved her mother-in-law, Naomi, and promised to stay with her no matter what. When Naomi heard that Bethlehem had food again, she moved back. Ruth went too and was soon gathering leftover grain in a farmer's field.

The farmer, kind and generous Boaz, noticed Ruth and spoke to her. Naomi praised God for that. "May he receive good from the Lord, Who has not kept His kindness from the living and dead," she said. "He is of our family" (Ruth 2:20). In those days, a widow's relative was expected to marry her to keep the family line going. Boaz was happy to do so.

Soon they had a baby, who grew up to have a baby, who grew up to have a baby who became king of Israel. And David had a family that a thousand years later produced Jesus, the Savior of the world!

God turned a poor foreign widow into the wife of a wealthy farmer. Then God made her a mom, and her family changed history. Wonder what He'll do with *your* life?

BIBLE ADVENTURE PRAYER STARTER

Lord, I want my life to make a difference like Ruth's did. Please do great things through me.

BIBLE ADVENTURE MEMORY VERSE

God is able to do much more than we ask or think through His power working in us.
EPHESIANS 3:20

JOHN THE APOSTLE:
JESUS' CLOSEST FRIEND

When Jesus had said this, He was troubled in heart. He told them in very plain words, saying, "For sure, I tell you, one of you is going to hand Me over to the leaders of the country." The followers began to look at each other. They did not know which one He was speaking of. One follower, whom Jesus loved, was beside Jesus. Simon Peter got this follower to look his way. He wanted him to ask Jesus which one He was speaking of.
JOHN 13:21–24

Did you know that Jesus had a best friend? It's true. While He lived on earth, Jesus' best friend was the disciple John.

Jesus loves *everyone*, enough to die on the cross to take the punishment for their sins. Anyone who believes in Him can receive the gift of salvation He offers. But some people get extra close to Jesus. When He was starting His ministry, Jesus chose twelve guys from the thousands and thousands of people in Galilee and Judea. Within that group, He spent the most time with three—Peter, James, and John. But it seems that John was Jesus' best buddy.

In the Bible's book of John, the name of John the Baptist appears several times. . .but the name of John the disciple never does. Many theologians—people who study the Bible super carefully—think John was just being humble. He chose not to mention his own name in the book he wrote. But sometimes he was part of the story, so he had to identify himself somehow. And he did that by calling himself "the follower whom Jesus loved."

A best friend is special. That person loves you all the time, no matter what. That person is always available, always ready to listen, always wanting to help. That person just makes things better by being in your life.

Jesus found that kind of person in John. Can He find that kind of person in you?

BIBLE ADVENTURE PRAYER STARTER

Jesus, You have done everything for me. I want to give my everything for You! Let's be best friends.

BIBLE ADVENTURE MEMORY VERSE

"I do not call you servants that I own anymore. A servant does not know what his owner is doing. I call you friends, because I have told you everything I have heard from My Father."
JOHN 15:15

JACOB:
WRESTLING WITH. . .GOD

Jacob was left alone. And a man fought with him until morning. When the man saw that he was not winning he touched the joint of Jacob's thigh. And Jacob's thigh was put out of joint while he fought with him. The man said, "Let me go. For the morning has come." But Jacob said, "I will not let you go unless you pray that good will come to me."
GENESIS 32:24–26

⁓⁓⁓⁓⁓⁓

Jacob wasn't a nice man. He cheated his brother, Esau, twice. He upset ten of his sons by making the eleventh his favorite. Given a chance, he usually made the most selfish decision.

But God still loved Jacob and used him for great things.

We can't always understand God's choices. He told the prophet Isaiah, "My thoughts are not your thoughts, and My ways are not your ways" (Isaiah 55:8). For His own good and wise reasons, God chose Jacob to start the nation of Israel. They would be God's special people who would bless everyone. How? By bringing Jesus, the Savior, into the world.

But thousands of years before that, God picked a sneaky, selfish man to be the patriarch—or founding father—of Israel. That was a new name God gave Jacob after a strange wrestling match near the Jabbok River. Jacob was alone when a mysterious man grabbed him. Jacob fought for his life, wrestling through the night. When dawn approached, the stranger said, "Let me go." Jacob refused, unless the man blessed him.

Selfish Jacob realized something during that fight: he wasn't wrestling just anyone, but God Himself! The "man" said, "Your name will no longer be Jacob, but Israel. For you have fought with God and with men, and have won" (Genesis 32:28). In awe, Jacob called the spot Peniel, meaning "face of God."

One lesson for us is the importance of wrestling in prayer. When you have a special need, hold tight to God. Keep holding on and say, "I won't let You go until You bless me!" If God blessed selfish Jacob, don't you think He'll bless you too?

BIBLE ADVENTURE PRAYER STARTER

Heavenly Father, I thank You for hearing my prayers. Here are the things I need Your help with:_____.

BIBLE ADVENTURE MEMORY VERSE

Jesus told them a picture-story to show that men should always pray and not give up.
LUKE 18:1

DANIEL:
GOOD DISOBEDIENCE

When Daniel knew that the king had written his name on this law, he went into his house where, in his upper room, he had windows open toward Jerusalem. There he got down on his knees three times each day, praying and giving thanks to his God, as he had done before.

DANIEL 6:10

~~~~~~~~~~~~~

Daniel survived a night with hungry lions. That miracle is what most people know about him. But it was an act of disobedience that got Daniel thrown to the lions. And in this case, disobedience was good.

Don't think you can just disobey anyone, anytime. God expects kids to obey their parents, and expects kids *and* parents to obey the laws of the land. But if someone orders you to do something sinful in God's eyes, you should say no.

In Daniel's time, bad people fooled the king into passing a stupid law. He ruled that nobody could pray to anyone but him for thirty days. Daniel, a faithful follower of God, wasn't going to obey that law. He kept praying to the one true God, like he always had.

Of course, the bad guys told on Daniel—that was their plan all along. And the king, who loved Daniel, had to follow his own foolish law. It said that anyone who disobeyed would be thrown to the lions.

You might think that obeying God would protect you from crazy situations like that. Not always. Daniel disobeyed a human law, and he faced a human punishment. Happily for him, God chose to shut the lions' mouths. Daniel came out of the den the next morning without a scratch from those hungry beasts. (And the lions *were* hungry. Happy that Daniel was okay, the king then threw the bad guys into the den—and even before they hit the floor, the lions jumped on them and crushed all their bones.)

God decides whether He'll rescue His people from the dangers of this life. He did that for Daniel. He doesn't do it for everyone. But when we stay faithful to Him, He'll make sure we're okay—either on earth or with Him in heaven forever.

BIBLE ADVENTURE PRAYER STARTER

Lord, I know You are strong enough to protect me from anything. Help me stay faithful to You in everything.

BIBLE ADVENTURE MEMORY VERSE

Keep me, O God, for I am safe in You.
PSALM 16:1

NICODEMUS:
WILLING TO LEARN

There was a man named Nicodemus. He was a proud religious law-keeper and a leader of the Jews. He came to Jesus at night and said, "Teacher, we know You have come from God to teach us. No one can do these powerful works You do unless God is with Him."

JOHN 3:1–2

Have you memorized John 3:16? It's probably the most famous verse in the whole Bible: "For God so loved the world that he gave his only Son. Whoever puts his trust in God's Son will not be lost but will have life that lasts forever."

Did you know that Jesus Himself spoke the words of John 3:16? And that He said them to a man named Nicodemus?

Nicodemus was an important person in Jesus' time and place. He was a Jewish religious leader, and most of the religious leaders hated Jesus. But Nicodemus was interested in what Jesus had to say, so he decided to make a visit and talk.

The Bible says Nicodemus visited Jesus at nighttime. We don't know exactly why, but it might be that Nicodemus didn't want the other leaders to know what he was doing. Still, Nicodemus went— and Jesus told him that he needed to be "born again" (John 3:3). That meant Nicodemus needed to believe in Jesus to give his spirit a fresh start. Only Jesus could clean up the sin inside Nicodemus—and the sin that's inside every one of us.

Did Nicodemus believe in Jesus right then? Or did he go home to think about what he'd heard? We don't know for sure what he did that night. But we do know that sometime later Nicodemus stood up for Jesus when the other religious leaders were insulting Him. And then, after Jesus was killed on the cross, Nicodemus helped take down His body and put it in a tomb. Both of those were brave things to do when so many people were against Jesus.

It seems that Nicodemus came to know the truth—"the Way and the Truth and the Life," as Jesus called Himself (John 14:6). This man's life was changed because he was willing to learn. Are you?

BIBLE ADVENTURE PRAYER STARTER

Lord Jesus, I want to learn more about You and Your salvation every day. Please teach me!

BIBLE ADVENTURE MEMORY VERSE

Learn to know our Lord Jesus Christ better. He is the One Who saves.
2 PETER 3:18

RAHAB:
A LIFE-AND-DEATH DECISION

"I have shown you kindness. So I beg of you, promise me by the Lord that you will show kindness to those of my father's house. . . . Save us from death."
JOSHUA 2:12–13

God had promised to give the Israelites a land called Canaan. Now they were right on the edge of Canaan, ready to move in. But something stood in the way: Jericho, a powerful city with thick walls. The Israelites had to get past Jericho to enter their promised land.

Israel's leader, Joshua, ordered two soldiers to sneak into Canaan and spy out the land. At Jericho they went to the house of a sinful woman named Rahab. It was right on the city's wall. Lots of men came and went from there, so they figured they wouldn't be noticed.

But they were! The king of Jericho wanted the Israelite spies, but Rahab had hidden them on her roof. When the king's men left, she got out a rope to let the spies down over the city wall.

Rahab had heard about Israel's God. She knew how strong He was—that He'd even divided the Red Sea when Moses led the people out of Egypt. She decided right then to serve God.

It was a life-and-death decision. If Jericho's

king found out she had helped enemy spies, she could be killed. If she stayed in the city when the Israelites attacked, she could be killed. By showing kindness to the spies, Rahab hoped the Israelites would show kindness in return. And they did.

The spies told Rahab that when Israel's army came, they would look for a red rope in her window. If she was in her house with her family, they would be saved.

Rahab did what she was told, and the spies did what they promised. Rahab and her family survived the destruction of Jericho. They became part of Israel. And she even became an ancestor of Jesus!

BIBLE ADVENTURE PRAYER STARTER

Heavenly Father, I thank You for Jesus, who saves me from the punishment of my sin and gives me eternal life!

BIBLE ADVENTURE MEMORY VERSE

"I have put in front of you today life and what is good, and death and what is bad. I tell you today to love the Lord your God. Walk in His ways."
DEUTERONOMY 30:15–16

MARK:
GETTING PAST OUR MISTAKES

Come to me here as soon as you can. Demas left me. He loved the things of this world and has gone to the city of Thessalonica. Crescens has gone to the city of Galatia. Titus has gone to the city of Dalmatia. Luke is the only one with me here. Bring Mark when you come. He is a help to me in this work.

2 TIMOTHY 4:9-11

~~~~~~~~

Have you ever made a big mistake? Mark sure did. One time, while he was on a missionary trip with the apostle Paul, Mark ran away. He bailed out. That doesn't sound very adventurous, does it?

Paul wasn't happy. Mark's bad decision even broke up Paul's missionary partnership with Barnabas. For their next trip, Barnabas wanted to try again with Mark, who was his cousin. The apostle basically said, "No way."

But over time, Mark got his act together. And by the end of Paul's life, when he was in jail for preaching about Jesus, he wrote the message above to his friend Timothy. Paul had seen another helper, Demas, also walk away from the ministry. Two other guys—Crescens and Titus—were still doing good work, but they were in other cities. Luke (who would write the New Testament books of Luke and Acts) was staying with Paul, but the old apostle really wanted to see *Mark* again. Paul was eager to spend some time with the guy who'd messed up years earlier! As Paul waited in prison for what would probably be a death sentence, he was thinking about the guy who'd gotten past a big mistake.

We all mess up sometimes. But if we ask, God always forgives. And then we will have new adventures to pursue.

BIBLE ADVENTURE PRAYER STARTER

Lord God, I want to do exciting things for You—but sometimes I mess up. I'm thankful for the example of Mark, who got past his mistakes. You used him in great ways, and You'll use me for big things too!

BIBLE ADVENTURE MEMORY VERSE

If we tell Him our sins, He is faithful and we can depend on Him to forgive us of our sins. He will make our lives clean from all sin.
1 JOHN 1:9

TIMOTHY:
GETTING PAST FEAR

If Timothy comes, receive him and help him so he will not be afraid. He is working for the Lord as I am. Everyone should respect him. Send him on his way to me in peace.

1 CORINTHIANS 16:10–11

~~~~~~

Of all the people who helped the apostle Paul, Timothy seems most important. Paul thought of Timothy as his "son in the Christian faith" (1 Timothy 1:2).

Timothy had a Christian mom and grandma who taught him about Jesus. They taught him well. Young Timothy was respected in his hometown of Lystra. Paul asked Timothy to travel with him to share the good news about Jesus. Timothy agreed.

Together they went from city to city. But sometimes Paul told Timothy to stay in a certain town—like Berea—to help the Christians grow. When Timothy felt they were okay, he left to try to catch up with Paul again. This happened several times: Paul and Timothy traveled together, separated to work in different cities, then found each other again.

Sounds like an adventure! Traveling to new places with a miracle-working apostle must be exciting.

Or maybe scary.

In a letter to Timothy, Paul mentioned his young

friend's stomach trouble, saying, "You are sick so often" (1 Timothy 5:23). In another letter, Paul remembered Timothy's tears when they parted (2 Timothy 1:4). Paul wrote to believers in Corinth to help Timothy "so he will not be afraid."

Life can be tough and scary. Some things—schoolwork, making friends, performing in music or sports—can be frightening. Sometimes people we love move away or get sick or die. Often the whole world feels broken, and it's hard to find joy.

Timothy probably had those feelings too. But he pressed forward and did what God wanted him to. Because of that, many people met Jesus. Hundreds, maybe thousands, who Timothy worked with are in heaven today. Millions who've learned from his story are either in heaven now or will be.

With God's help, Timothy got past his fear. You can pray for that too. Just imagine how God might use *you*.

BIBLE ADVENTURE PRAYER STARTER

Father God, give me courage when I'm afraid. I want to press forward like Timothy and accomplish great things for You.

BIBLE ADVENTURE MEMORY VERSE

There is no fear in love. Perfect love puts fear out of our hearts.
1 John 4:18

MOSES:
ADVENTUREMAN!

The Lord said to Moses, "Put out your hand toward the sky. And there will be darkness over the land of Egypt, a darkness people will feel." So Moses put out his hand toward the sky. And there was darkness in all the land of Egypt for three days.
Exodus 10:21–22

Seems like everyone loves superhero movies. Maybe that's because, deep down, we'd all enjoy soaring through the air like a bird. Or we'd like to pick up a semitruck without breaking a sweat. Or, best of all, we'd love to make things better for people in danger or need.

In Bible times, Moses was that superhero.

When you read about the ten terrible plagues on Egypt, you see Moses showing off some crazy powers. To convince Pharaoh to set God's people free from their slavery, Moses (let's call him "Adventureman") made wild things happen:

Second plague: *Boom!* Frogs cover Egypt. Maybe that sounds funny, until you realize there were frogs in people's beds and ovens, even their bread dough. And when the frogs died off, the whole country stunk.

Fifth plague: *Bam!* Egypt's farm animals die. No more milk or fresh meat.

Seventh plague: *Kapow!* Moses raises his hand and thunder, lightning, and hail rock Egypt. This powerful storm wiped out Egypt's farm fields.

Ninth plague: *Wham!* Heavy black darkness falls over the land.

Tenth plague: *Whoa. . .*every firstborn child of Egypt dies.

Can you imagine having that kind of power?

Well, not even Moses had that kind of power. The plagues on Egypt were *God's* power coming *through* Moses. He was only doing what God told him to do.

And that's something we all can do. We all can obey God's Word, doing what the Bible says. We all can listen for His Spirit, speaking quietly to our hearts—and then follow His leading. Whatever job God has for us, exciting or dull, happy or sad, we can do it in His strength. Just be willing.

BIBLE ADVENTURE PRAYER STARTER

Heavenly Father, You are strong! Please show Your strength through me. Help me to help others in whatever they need—and especially to introduce them to Your Son, Jesus Christ.

BIBLE ADVENTURE MEMORY VERSE

I can do all things because Christ gives me the strength.
PHILIPPIANS 4:13

EZEKIEL:
CATCHING GOD'S VISION

Sitting on the throne was what looked like a man. Then I saw that there was something like shining brass from the center of his body and up to his head. It looked like fire all around within it. And from the center of his body and down to his feet I saw something like fire. There was a bright light shining all around Him.
EZEKIEL 1:26–27

Ever hear the phrase "catch the vision"? People say that to urge you to join a big, important project. The "vision" is the goal. When you "catch" it, you're excited to help out.

Ezekiel "caught the vision," in more ways than one. He joined a big, important project—telling God's words to sinful Israel. And he actually *saw* visions, strange moving pictures that God showed him. Can you imagine seeing what Ezekiel described?

I saw there were very many bones, and they were very dry. He said to me, "Son of man, can these bones live?" I answered, "O Lord God, only You know that." He said to me, "Speak in My name over these bones. . . ."
So I spoke as I was told. And as I spoke,

there was a noise, the sound of bones hit-
ting against each other. The bones came to-
gether, bone to bone. . . . Flesh had grown,
and they were covered with skin. But there
was no breath in them. Then He said to me,
"Speak to the breath in My name, son of
man. Tell the breath, 'The Lord God says,
"Come from the four winds, O breath, and
breathe on these dead bodies to make
them come to life." ' " So I spoke as I had
been told. The breath came into them, and
they came to life and stood on their feet.
They were a large army.

EZEKIEL 37:2–4, 7–10

Ezekiel saw visions of God Himself and of the
spiritually dead Israelites coming back to life.

There are "dead people," who don't know
Jesus, everywhere. Can you "catch the vision" of
introducing them to the one who gives life?

BIBLE ADVENTURE PRAYER STARTER

Lord, I want to catch Your vision—
to see people saved by Jesus!

BIBLE ADVENTURE MEMORY VERSE

"This is life that lasts forever. It is
to know You, the only true God, and to
know Jesus Christ Whom You have sent."

JOHN 17:3

MARTHA:
ADVENTURES IN SERVING

Mary sat at the feet of Jesus and listened to all He said. Martha was working hard getting the supper ready.
LUKE 10:39–40

~~~~~~~~~~~~~~~~~~

Some people love to help out. If there's a yard that needs mowed, they'll mow it. If there's a cake that needs baked, they'll bake it. If there's a bill that needs paid, they'll pay it.

Do you know anyone like that? Maybe this describes *you.* God wants everyone to be helpful, but some people are especially good at it. Helping is a "spiritual gift," something God gives certain people so they can bless others (1 Corinthians 12:28).

Jesus' friend Martha was a worker. Along with her sister Mary and brother Lazarus, she loved to have Jesus visit. When He was on His way, Martha started cooking, cleaning. . .and fussing.

One time Jesus was in the house and Martha was still working. Mary, though, was just sitting close to Jesus, listening to everything He said. Martha got frustrated. She was doing all the work and Mary was just relaxing with the guest. *It's not fair!* she probably thought.

Finally, Martha complained to Jesus. "Do You see that my sister is not helping me? Tell her to help me" (Luke 10:40).

Jesus started His answer by repeating His good friend's name: "Martha, Martha." When people do that, they're kind of saying, "You know I love and appreciate you, but I need you to calm down and listen to something important." Then Jesus said, "You are worried and troubled about many things. Only a few things are important, even just one. Mary has chosen the good thing" (Luke 10:41–42).

What Jesus meant was that spending time with Him—listening to Him and talking with Him—was even more important than doing things for Him. Martha loved to work, which is great. But sometimes her work kept her away from the most important thing—knowing Jesus as well as she could.

We should certainly do good things for Jesus. But let's be sure to spend time with Him first.

BIBLE ADVENTURE PRAYER STARTER

Dear Jesus, I want to serve You well— but first I need to know You better. May I spend good, quiet time just listening to You.

BIBLE ADVENTURE MEMORY VERSE

"Come to Me, all of you who work and have heavy loads. I will give you rest."
MATTHEW 11:28

NAAMAN:
ARGUE OR OBEY

Naaman came with his horses and his war-wagons, and stood at the door of Elisha's house. Elisha sent a man to him, saying, "Go and wash in the Jordan seven times. And your flesh will be made well and you will be clean."

2 KINGS 5:9-10

~~~~~~~~~~

Naaman was a tough army commander from Syria. He made battle plans, ordered his soldiers into war, and won many victories. But there was one battle he couldn't win. Naaman had a skin disease called leprosy, and nothing he did could change that.

A young servant girl of Naaman's wife had a helpful idea, though. The girl was an Israelite, and she had been kidnapped by Syrian soldiers. She ended up working in Naaman's house. She must have been very kind, because she went to Naaman's wife and said, "I wish that my owner's husband were with the man of God who is in Samaria! Then he would heal his bad skin disease" (2 Kings 5:3).

Naaman got permission from Syria's king to go look for "the man of God," Elisha. But when the tough army commander reached the prophet's house, Elisha didn't come out to see him. He just sent a servant out with a message: "Go and wash in the Jordan seven times. And your flesh will be made well and you will be clean."

Naaman had expected Elisha to do something dramatic. The big, strong soldier was angry and decided the rivers of Syria would be just as good to wash in as Israel's muddy little Jordan.

Happily for Naaman, he had servants who were as wise as his wife's servant. They said, "If the man of God had told you to do some great thing, would you not have done it?" (2 Kings 5:13). They urged Naaman to do the one simple thing Elisha had commanded. Naaman listened to them and did what Elisha said. And he was completely healed!

Every day we all have a choice to make: When God gives a command, will we argue or obey? Arguing gets us nowhere. Obedience is always rewarded, either in this life or in heaven to come.

BIBLE ADVENTURE PRAYER STARTER

Heavenly Father, help me always to obey
You, immediately and cheerfully!

BIBLE ADVENTURE MEMORY VERSE

Obey the Word of God. If you hear only and
do not act, you are only fooling yourself.
JAMES 1:22

PAUL:
BULLETPROOF

I have a desire to leave this world to be with Christ, which is much better. But it is more important for you that I stay. I am sure I will live to help you grow and be happy in your faith.

PHILIPPIANS 1:23–25

~~~~~~~~~~

Okay, so there weren't any bullets in Bible times. The title above just means the apostle had miracle protection throughout his life. To use a big word, he was *indestructible*. Nothing could kill him until his work for God was done.

Paul dodged one "bullet" after another. Early in his ministry, he was almost stoned to death. When he healed a man who couldn't walk, the people of Lystra thought Paul was a god until Jews from other cities turned them against him. Before long, they were throwing stones at Paul. They dragged his body out of the city, but he was soon back on his feet, preaching again!

Many Jewish people hated Paul's preaching. They didn't believe Jesus was God's Son, and they didn't want Paul saying that—especially since Paul had once believed like they did. One time several Jews promised not to eat until they had killed Paul. Their plan failed, but we don't know if they eventually starved to death.

Toward the end of his life, Paul was sailing to Rome for a trial before the emperor, Caesar. The apostle had been accused of so many things that he wanted to take his case to the highest authority—and tell Caesar about Jesus. On the way, a terrible storm blew up, but God sent an angel to say Paul and his 275 shipmates would survive. The boat was destroyed, but everyone swam to shore on the island of Malta. There, building a fire to keep warm, Paul was bit by a venomous snake! That didn't hurt him either. (You can read about this in Acts 27 and 28.)

Paul's life was totally in God's hands. Until God decided it was Paul's time to die, he was bulletproof. That's true for you too. There's no need to fear trouble or death in this world. Do what God calls you to do, and trust Him completely to keep you safe.

BIBLE ADVENTURE PRAYER STARTER

Lord, it's a scary world, but You are in complete control. Give me peace and confidence like You gave Paul.

BIBLE ADVENTURE MEMORY VERSE

Even if I walk into trouble,
You will keep my life safe.
PSALM 138:7

SOLOMON:
ASK FOR ANYTHING!

The Lord came to Solomon in a special dream in Gibeon during the night. God said, "Ask what you wish Me to give you."
1 KINGS 3:5

~~~~~~~~~~~

Solomon already had a lot going for him. He was a child of Israel's greatest king. And he was the son chosen to follow David on Israel's throne.

But once the young man became king himself, he had a chance for even more—far more. God visited Solomon to say, basically, "Ask for anything!"

If you had that opportunity, what would you want? Lots of money? Popularity? Good looks? Talent to sing or act or play sports?

Solomon didn't ask for anything like that. Instead, he said to God, "You have shown great loving-kindness to Your servant David my father because he was faithful and right and good and pure in heart before You. . . . O Lord my God, You have made Your servant king in place of my father David. But I am only a little child. I do not know how to start or finish. . . . So give Your servant an understanding heart to judge Your people and know the difference between good and bad" (1 Kings 3:6–7, 9).

In a word, Solomon asked for *wisdom*. And that was a smart choice.

God was pleased with Solomon's answer. "You have asked this," the Lord said, "and have not asked for long life for yourself. You have not asked for riches, or for the life of those who hate you. But you have asked for understanding to know what is right" (1 Kings 3:11). Asking for wisdom was wise—and God said He would reward Solomon by giving him good things that he had *not* requested. "I give you both riches and honor," God told Solomon. "So there will be no king like you all your days" (verse 13).

Solomon's request is one we can all make. And God will be happy to answer. Ask Him for wisdom and watch what He does!

BIBLE ADVENTURE PRAYER STARTER

Lord, I want a lot of things—but I need wisdom. Please show me the right thing to do in every situation.

BIBLE ADVENTURE MEMORY VERSE

If you do not have wisdom, ask God for it. He is always ready to give it to you and will never say you are wrong for asking.
JAMES 1:5

JOSEPH, SON OF JACOB:
DON'T BRAG

Joseph had a dream. When he told it to his brothers, they hated him even more.
GENESIS 37:5

~~~~~~~

Even as a kid, you sometimes get to enjoy big adventures. Maybe you score the winning basket for your team. Maybe you create the prize-winning cupcakes in a bake-off. Maybe you get to go mountain climbing or skydiving. All of those things are great! If you experience such things, thank God—but don't brag.

Boasting got a teenager named Joseph in trouble. He turned out to be a great man, but God had to work around young Joseph's cockiness. Here's what happened.

Joseph's dad was Jacob, grandson of Abraham. This family was God's special people, the nation of Israel that would one day produce Jesus, Savior of the world. Though Jacob was an important man, he sure wasn't perfect. He had twelve boys by four women, and Joseph was his favorite son from his favorite wife. If you're thinking, *That can't be good*, give yourself a pat on the back!

Daddy gave Joseph a special coat that showed his ten older brothers how "special" he was. They hated him for it. Then, when God showed Joseph future things through dreams, the boy quickly told his brothers. What did he dream? That the older brothers would one day bow down to Joseph! The hatred rose into the danger zone, and the older boys were ready to kill. They ended up selling Joseph into slavery.

In the end, though, his dreams came true. By a chain of miracles, Joseph became the second most important ruler in Egypt. When a famine in Judah forced the older brothers out looking to buy food, they found themselves bowing before a powerful Egyptian official. . .who turned out to be their little brother!

Joseph knew everything that had happened was within God's good plan (Genesis 50:20). But he might have regretted his youthful boasting that had upset his brothers so badly.

When good things happen, you don't have to hide them. Just be sure you don't brag. Bragging only pushes people away.

BIBLE ADVENTURE PRAYER STARTER

Lord God, I'm grateful for my blessings. Help me not to brag, since I know that every good thing comes from You.

BIBLE ADVENTURE MEMORY VERSE

"If anyone is going to be proud of anything, he should be proud of the Lord."
1 CORINTHIANS 1:31

ELIZABETH:
"GOD CAN DO ALL THINGS"

"See, your cousin Elizabeth, as old as she is, is going to give birth to a child. She was not able to have children before, but now she is in her sixth month. For God can do all things."

LUKE 1:36–37

~~~~~~~~~

Elizabeth was sad. She was embarrassed. She was ashamed.

What had she done wrong? Nothing. But she had never been able to have a baby. In the time and place Elizabeth lived, women were expected to have kids. If they didn't, they were looked down on.

Elizabeth was married to a priest. Zacharias worked in God's temple in Jerusalem. Four hundred years had passed since God last spoke to His people, through the prophet Malachi. Suddenly God's angel appeared to Zacharias. The old priest was frightened, but the angel said, "Zacharias, do not be afraid. Your prayer has been heard. Your wife Elizabeth will give birth to a son" (Luke 1:13). That son would be called John. Today we know him as John the Baptist.

The angel, Gabriel, told Zacharias that John would be "great in the sight of the Lord" and "get people ready for the Lord" (Luke 1:15, 17). "The Lord is Jesus, who would soon be born to Elizabeth's younger relative, Mary. Gabriel visited her too, telling Mary that her own miracle baby would be called "Son of the Most High" (Luke 1:32).

Gabriel wanted Mary to trust that God could and would do what He'd said. So he told Mary, "See, your cousin Elizabeth, old as she is, is going to give birth to a child. . . . For God can do all things."

Everything happened just as Gabriel said. Elizabeth had a baby named John, Mary had baby Jesus, and the two boys became great. Elizabeth's son pointed people to Mary's Son, who lived and died to offer salvation to everyone.

Elizabeth's sadness had an end. Her salvation, through Jesus, is forever. That's true for all who follow Him. The hard things of this world will stop. The perfect happiness of heaven will go on and on. Because God can do all things.

BIBLE ADVENTURE PRAYER STARTER

Lord, please change my sadness to joy, my embarrassment to celebration. I know You can do all things!

BIBLE ADVENTURE MEMORY VERSE

Save me by Your name, O God.
And stand with me by Your power.
PSALM 54:1

PETER:
FISHERMAN? FISHER OF MEN!

Jesus was walking by the Sea of Galilee. He saw two brothers. They were Simon (his other name was Peter) and Andrew, his brother. They were putting a net into the sea for they were fishermen. Jesus said to them, "Follow Me. I will make you fish for men!" At once they left their nets and followed Him.

MATTHEW 4:18–20

～～～～～

God likes it when people work hard. The very first person, Adam, was supposed to "work the ground and care for it" (Genesis 2:15). It doesn't matter what job you have, whether other people think it's "important" or not. Wherever God puts you, He wants you to do things well.

Before Peter met Jesus, he was a fisherman. So was his brother Andrew. So were their business partners, James and John, another set of brothers. Their kind of fishing was hard work. They were often out in the hot sun. They had to repair their boats and mend their nets. Sometimes they didn't catch anything. Other times the nets were loaded with heavy fish. When that happened, they had to clean and deliver the fish, a messy, smelly job.

When Jesus said, "Follow Me," Peter seemed happy to leave his nets behind. He obeyed right away. Jesus had a new job for Peter, and He called it "fishing for men." Peter had worked hard at catching fish to make people happy at dinnertime. Now Jesus wanted him to catch people to make God happy for all time!

Peter had a new "calling"—Jesus made him a preacher of the gospel, the good news about salvation. It's great to be a preacher or a missionary or a Christian singer. If that's what God wants for you, study, practice, and do your very best. But if God wants you as a schoolteacher, or a firefighter, or a home decorator, that's great too. Doing any job well honors Jesus and gives you opportunities to talk about Him. You can fish for people anywhere, anytime.

BIBLE ADVENTURE PRAYER STARTER

Lord Jesus, I wonder what job You'll have for me when I grow up. Show me how to get ready—whatever it is, I want to do it well!

BIBLE ADVENTURE MEMORY VERSE

Whatever work you do, do it with all your heart. Do it for the Lord and not for men.
COLOSSIANS 3:23

NOAH:
A WHOLE NEW WORLD

In the year 601, in the first month, on the first day of the month, the water was dried up from the earth. Then Noah took the covering off the large boat, and looked out and saw that the earth was dry. . . . Then God said to Noah, "Go out of the boat, you and your wife and your sons and your sons' wives with you."
GENESIS 8:13, 15–16

~~~~~~~~~~

Imagine being Noah. He was the only good man on earth when God told him to build the ark. In that big boat, Noah and his family, along with pairs of all the animals, would survive a worldwide flood. God was wiping sin from the earth and starting over. Noah's family would step out of the ark into a whole new world.

It was like an artist's blank canvas. Noah could paint whatever picture he wanted. He got off to a great start by building an altar to God. That was an act of worship. Noah knew that God had created the world and set the rules for it. God had the right to wipe out sin and start over. And God could tell Noah and his family exactly what to do next: "Have many children, and cover the earth" (Genesis 9:1). They obeyed, and the new world began to fill up again.

But this world wasn't perfect either. Noah himself made a mistake by getting drunk one night. And his son Ham messed up by not helping Noah as he should have. Over time, the new world became a lot like the old one, full of sinful people who disrespected God.

That describes our world today. Many people—actually, *most* people—fight against God. They don't want to do what He says. They don't even want to believe He exists! But God is real, and He is powerful, and He is planning a totally new world for all who believe in His Son, Jesus. That world *will* be perfect, and nothing will ever go wrong there.

BIBLE ADVENTURE PRAYER STARTER

Lord God, I look forward to Your perfect new world. Help me to invite many others to join us in it.

BIBLE ADVENTURE MEMORY VERSE

"God will take away all their tears. There will be no more death or sorrow or crying or pain. All the old things have passed away."
REVELATION 21:4

STEPHEN:
"I SEE JESUS!"

The Jews and religious leaders listened to Stephen. Then they became angry and began to grind their teeth at him. He was filled with the Holy Spirit. As he looked up to heaven, he saw the shining-greatness of God and Jesus standing at the right side of God. He said, "See! I see heaven open and the Son of Man standing at the right side of God!"
ACTS 7:54–56

~~~~~~~~~~~~~~~~

Stephen's adventure is like a roller coaster—up and down and up again.

After Jesus died on the cross, came back to life, and returned to heaven, His church grew. Many people believed the good news of salvation and followed Jesus.

In Jerusalem the apostles decided to find men to care for the growing church. Peter, John, Matthew, and the rest of the twelve disciples would pray and teach. Men called "deacons" would do things like take food to the widows.

Stephen was one of the first deacons. He was a good man, "full of faith and full of the Holy Spirit" (Acts 6:5). By God's power, Stephen even performed miracles! And he spoke powerfully about Jesus.

Jewish leaders who hated Jesus hated Stephen too. They told lies to get him in trouble and brought him in front of the chief priest. Stephen boldly told the religious leaders even *more* about Jesus! When Stephen said, "I see heaven open and the Son of Man standing at the right side of God," the religious leaders went crazy. They dragged Stephen outside and threw stones at him to kill him.

As he was dying, Stephen followed Jesus' example, praying, "Lord, do not hold this sin against them" (Acts 7:60). Within seconds, Stephen was with Jesus in heaven!

Jesus' enemies then turned against the other Christians around Jerusalem. Many had to run away from the city. But you know what? They took the good news of Jesus to other people in other places. What happened to Stephen, sad as it was, changed many lives for good. Because of his faithfulness, other people could also say, "I see Jesus!"

BIBLE ADVENTURE PRAYER STARTER

Lord Jesus, You gave Your life for me. Help me, like Stephen, to follow You without fear. I want others to know You too.

BIBLE ADVENTURE MEMORY VERSE

I hope to honor Christ with my body if it be by my life or by my death.
PHILIPPIANS 1:20

GAIUS:
SUPPORTING THE ADVENTURE

Timothy, my helper, greets you. Lucius and Jason and Sosipater from my family say hello also. . . . Gaius is the man taking care of me. The church meets here in his house. He greets you.

ROMANS 16:21, 23

~~~~~~~~~~~~

Life won't always *feel* like an adventure. Sometimes you're stuck in a boring class at school. Rainy days mess up your outdoor plans. When you become an adult, you'll have times when your job is dull and frustrating. Don't believe it? Ask any grown-up, and they'll tell you it's true.

But whatever's going on, wherever you are, you can still support the great adventure of the Christian faith. That's what a man named Gaius did.

We don't know a lot about Gaius. The name shows up only five times in the Bible, and it seems like it belonged to two or three different guys. The one in Romans 16 probably came to know Jesus through the apostle Paul's preaching. We know for sure, from today's scripture, that he was taking care of Paul when the apostle wrote a very important letter to Christians in Rome. We now call that letter the book of Romans.

Do you see what happened there? God used

Gaius in a quiet but remarkable way. Because Gaius was willing to help Paul, Paul could write this letter. And because of this letter called Romans, an untold number of lives have been affected for good. Gaius played a part in the faith of every Christian who's ever learned from the book of Romans.

There's nothing boring about that!

BIBLE ADVENTURE PRAYER STARTER

Heavenly Father, You can accomplish amazing things with anyone. I don't have to be an apostle Paul to serve You and others—I can also be a Gaius, someone who just helps out where needed. Thank You for giving me opportunities. May many people come to know You because of my faithful service.

BIBLE ADVENTURE MEMORY VERSE

Do not let yourselves get tired of doing good. If we do not give up, we will get what is coming to us at the right time. Because of this, we should do good to everyone. For sure, we should do good to those who belong to Christ.
GALATIANS 6:9–10

JEHOSHEBA:
ONE BRAVE CHOICE

When Ahaziah's mother Athaliah saw that her son was dead, she got up and killed all the king's children. But King Joram's daughter Jehosheba, Ahaziah's sister, took Joash the son of Ahaziah. She stole him away from the king's sons who were being killed, and put him and his nurse in the bedroom. They hid him from Athaliah, and he was not killed.

2 KINGS 11:1–2

Think you'd like to be part of a royal family? To have the king and queen as your parents and live in a fancy palace? To ride in an expensive carriage—or car or jet, these days? To have everyone know who you are and think you're important?

Maybe. Just watch out for the royal intrigue.

Intrigue (pronounced *IN-treegh*) happens when other people want to replace you as royalty. They work behind the scenes to make themselves rulers. It can be really nasty, as a woman named Athaliah proves.

She was the mother of Judah's king Ahaziah. But when he died in battle, she decided to take his place by killing all the rest of her family! That's where Jehosheba comes in.

If you haven't heard of Jehosheba, don't be embarrassed. She's in only two verses of the whole

Bible. . .and in some translations her name is spelled two ways. (She's called Jehoshabeath in 2 Chronicles 22:11.)

What we know about Jehosheba is small. But the good thing she did was huge: When Athaliah was wiping out everyone else who could follow Ahaziah, Jehosheba jumped into action. She grabbed Ahaziah's baby son, Joash, who was her nephew. She hid him from Athaliah so he wasn't killed.

Six years later, Athaliah was killed and seven-year-old Joash became king! Since he was so young, a priest named Jehoiada guided him. As long as Jehoiada lived, Joash obeyed God and led his kingdom well. That could not have happened without Jehosheba's courage.

Today, ask God to help *you* do the right thing when the opportunity arises. You never know what one brave choice might accomplish.

BIBLE ADVENTURE PRAYER STARTER

Heavenly Father, please show me opportunities to do right, and then give me courage to do what I should.

BIBLE ADVENTURE MEMORY VERSE

Religion that is pure and good before God the Father is to help children who have no parents and to care for women whose husbands have died.

JAMES 1:27

ABRAHAM:
GOING PLACES

The Lord said to Abram, "Leave your country, your family and your father's house, and go to the land that I will show you. And I will make you a great nation. I will bring good to you. I will make your name great. . . . Good will come to all the families of the earth because of you."
GENESIS 12:1–3

Some people love to travel. They want to see new places, meet new people, try new foods, and learn new things. Other people would rather stick around home. They prefer things that are familiar. Which kind of person are you?

We don't know if Abraham was the type of guy who loved adventure. But when God offered one, Abraham took it!

Called Abram at first, he lived in a place that would later be known as Babylon. The people there worshipped false gods.

For some reason, Abram's father, Terah, decided to move his family to Canaan. That's the "promised land" that God would one day give to Abram. But God hadn't yet spoken to Abram, and Terah never reached Canaan. The family stopped at a place called Haran and settled down.

That's where the true God introduced Himself

to Abram with the words of the scripture above. God wanted Abram to leave Haran and many of his relatives and friends. Abram was just supposed to follow God "to the land that I will show you."

Maybe that was exciting. Maybe it was scary. Either way, Abram obeyed: "He left his home without knowing where he was going" (Hebrews 11:8).

Abram did what God said, and God did what He promised. He made Abram into a great nation, the people of Israel. God made Abram's name great. (Think about it: we're still talking about him four thousand years later!) And God brought good to all people through Abram. How? By sending Jesus to earth through Abram's family, the nation of Israel.

None of that would have happened if Abram had decided to stay in Haran. But when he obeyed God by faith, amazing things followed. When God gives you an opportunity, take it!

BIBLE ADVENTURE PRAYER STARTER

Heavenly Father, help me to recognize the opportunities You offer—and then follow You in faith!

BIBLE ADVENTURE MEMORY VERSE

Because Abraham had faith, he obeyed God when God called him to leave his home.
HEBREWS 11:8

JOHN THE BAPTIST:
CHANGE THE WORLD

The Word of God came to John the Baptist, the son of Zacharias. John was in the desert. He went into all the country around the Jordan River. He preached that people should be baptized because they were sorry for their sins and had turned from them, and they would be forgiven. The early preacher Isaiah wrote these words: "His voice calls out in the desert. 'Make the way ready for the Lord. Make the road straight for Him!... And all men will see God saving people from the punishment of their sins.'"

Luke 3:2–4, 6

Lots of people say they want to "change the world." Maybe you've even said that yourself.

For most of us, "change the world" means we do good where we are, helping the people around us. Our world tends to be small, and that's okay.

But John the Baptist really did change the world—the whole world. How? By getting people ready to meet Jesus. Hundreds of years before John was born, the prophet Isaiah said God would send someone to do that important job. That "someone" was John.

He was an interesting guy. A miracle baby, born to an old priest and his wife who had never been able to have children. An outdoorsy guy who lived in the desert, wore rough clothes, and ate locusts. A powerful speaker when God told him it was time to start sharing his message. People came from all around to hear John preach and get baptized by him.

But just as soon as Jesus appeared, John pointed everyone to Him. "See!" John exclaimed. "The Lamb of God Who takes away the sin of the world!" (John 1:29).

That's the message that truly changes the world. And it's a message *you* can share, just like John did. Can you think of someone who needs to hear about Jesus?

BIBLE ADVENTURE PRAYER STARTER

Lord Jesus, John the Baptist got people ready to meet You. I'd like to do the same! Please give me the words and the courage to share the good news about You.

BIBLE ADVENTURE MEMORY VERSE

I am not ashamed of the Good News. It is the power of God. It is the way He saves men from the punishment of their sins if they put their trust in Him.
ROMANS 1:16

ANDREW:
ADVENTURES IN MULTIPLICATION

One of His followers was Andrew, Simon Peter's brother. He said to Jesus, "There is a boy here who has five loaves of barley bread and two small fish. What is that for so many people?"
JOHN 6:8-9

~~~~~~~~~~~~~~~~~

Some kids love math. Others hate it. Everyone has to learn it.

Jesus' disciples once got a miraculous lesson in multiplication. You might remember how Jesus took a boy's small lunch to make a feast for a huge crowd—five thousand men and all the women and children with them. But did you know it was Peter's brother Andrew who brought that boy to Jesus?

People followed Jesus everywhere He went. They liked to hear His teaching, even if they didn't always understand or believe it. They loved the fact that He healed them of their physical problems.

One time Jesus looked over a crowd and asked His disciple Philip where they could get enough bread for everyone. Philip said the disciples couldn't scrape up the money for each person to get even a tiny bite.

That's when Andrew said, "There is a boy here who has five loaves of barley bread and two small fish." It seems like Andrew thought Jesus might do something surprising with that little lunch. But then

Andrew said, "What is that for so many people?"

He didn't realize that Jesus' "multiplication table" could make a small lunch thousands of times larger! Jesus had the people sit on the grass, then he took the little lunch and prayed. He started breaking the bread and fish and handing them to the disciples to deliver to the people. Jesus kept breaking and handing, and the disciples kept delivering—over and over again, until everyone had eaten as much as they wanted.

That's the way our God works. The Father, through Jesus the Son and His Holy Spirit, can do anything. And He loves to bless His children! If you follow Jesus, know that God will always give you what you need. Many times He'll also give you things you want. He's a very good Father.

BIBLE ADVENTURE PRAYER STARTER

Heavenly Father, I know You can do anything.
Thank You for all the good You give me.
Help me always to thank and trust You.

BIBLE ADVENTURE MEMORY VERSE

God can give you all you need.
He will give you more than enough.
2 CORINTHIANS 9:8

JESUS:
DOING THE UNEXPECTED

A woman of Samaria came to get water.
Jesus said to her, "Give Me a drink.". . . The
woman of Samaria said to Him, "You are a
Jew. I am of Samaria. Why do You ask me
for a drink when the Jews have nothing
to do with the people of Samaria?"
JOHN 4:7, 9

Want to stand out from the crowd? Do the unexpected—the unexpectedly *good*. Jesus set the example.

He was Jewish. In Jesus' time, most Jews disliked a group of people called Samaritans. They were named after Samaria, a place that had once been Jewish. But over the years, the Samaritans had married outsiders and taken on different beliefs. The "pure" Jews looked down on them.

So it was unusual for Jesus even to travel through Samaria. And it was really surprising when He spoke to a Samaritan. It was almost shocking that Jesus talked with a Samaritan *woman*—Jewish men just didn't do things like that!

But Jesus did. And He did the unexpected so that anyone—whatever their background—could come to know His heavenly Father.

When Jesus asked this woman for a drink from

the well, He was planning to tell her about salvation. The well water would take care of her thirst for a short time. But the "living water" Jesus offered would satisfy her soul forever.

The woman knew enough about Jewish beliefs to be expecting the Messiah, or Christ, God's Savior for the world. Jesus told her, "I am the Christ, the One talking with you!" (John 4:26).

She was so excited that she ran back to her town and started telling people, "Come see a Man Who told me everything I ever did! Can this be the Christ?" (John 4:29). Her neighbors believed her message and invited Jesus to stay in their town. He did, for two days—and many of those Samaritans put their trust in Him.

Doing the unexpected—the unexpectedly kind, the unexpectedly generous, the unexpectedly forgiving—is a great way to point people to God. Can you do something like that today?

BIBLE ADVENTURE PRAYER STARTER

Jesus, I want to be like You—
doing the unexpected so people
can come to know Your Father.

BIBLE ADVENTURE MEMORY VERSE

If the one who hates you is hungry,
feed him. If he is thirsty, give him water.
PROVERBS 25:21

MARY MAGDALENE:
FRIEND TO THE END

*The mother of Jesus and her sister Mary,
the wife of Cleophas, were standing near
the cross. Mary Magdalene was there also.*
JOHN 19:25

~~~~~~~~~~~

If you were describing the perfect friend, what would that person be like? Words such as *kind*, *helpful*, and *encouraging* come to mind. Now imagine if that "perfect friend" was willing to *die* for you—then you'd be describing Jesus!

When He lived on earth, Jesus was the perfect friend. He never treated anyone selfishly. He never gossiped or envied. He always showed love and grace to all His followers—though they often failed Him.

When Jesus was arrested, all His male disciples "left Him and ran away" (Matthew 26:56). But the *women* who followed Jesus were very faithful. His mother was standing nearby as He hung on the cross. So was Jesus' dear friend Mary Magdalene.

She had followed Jesus on the long walk from His home in Galilee to Jerusalem, where He was crucified. Mary had provided money for Jesus and His disciples, and "cared for Him" in other ways (Matthew 27:55). She saw Jesus nailed to the cross and watched Him suffer for hours. Then she heard Him say, "It is finished" (John 19:30) as He died.

Mary was heartbroken, but she stayed by her friend and Lord as long as she could. She followed along as the brave and faithful Joseph and Nicodemus carried Jesus' body to the tomb. And after the opening was covered with a heavy stone, Mary *still* stayed as close as she could.

Finally, she forced herself to go home and obey the Sabbath, the Jewish day of rest. But as soon as the sun rose on Sunday morning, she was heading back to Jesus' tomb for a final act of love. Mary was going to put good-smelling spices on His body to cover up the smell of death.

But Jesus was alive again! And the first person who got to see Him was Mary Magdalene. She was a friend to the end—but for Christians there really is no "end." Death is just the door to a perfect forever with Jesus.

BIBLE ADVENTURE PRAYER STARTER

Jesus, thank You for being the perfect friend. Help me always to be true to You.

BIBLE ADVENTURE MEMORY VERSE

"The one who stays true to the end will be saved."
MATTHEW 24:13

ZACCHEUS:
MAKING THINGS RIGHT

Zaccheus stood up and said to the Lord, "Lord, see! Half of what I own I will give to poor people. And if I have taken money from anyone in a wrong way, I will pay him back four times as much."

LUKE 19:8

~~~~~~~~~~~~~~~~~~~~~

Want to make the world a better place? Admit when you're wrong and do everything you can to make things right. That's what the tax collector Zaccheus did, and Jesus said it proved the "wee little man" was saved.

Zaccheus was short—so short that he couldn't see over other people watching Jesus walk through Jericho. Since helicopters weren't around yet, Zaccheus did what he could to get a better view. He climbed a tree.

Jesus was popular. He went from place to place preaching, healing people, and doing miracles like feeding thousands with one small lunch. Many wanted to see Him, and from a tree limb, Zaccheus got his own view of Jesus. But Jesus also saw Zaccheus—and He said, "Come down at once. I must stay in your house today" (Luke 19:5).

The little man was thrilled. Other people were unhappy. They grumbled among themselves, saying, "He is going to stay with a man who is known to be a sinner" (Luke 19:7).

Nobody likes to pay taxes, so Zaccheus' job made him unpopular. But he had also charged people more money than he should have. He became rich by cheating! People in Jericho called Zaccheus "a sinner."

But *everyone* is a sinner, and Jesus said He came "to look for and to save from the punishment of sin those who are lost" (Luke 19:10). When Jesus found Zaccheus, the little man admitted he'd done wrong. He promised to give half of all he owned to poor people. And he said that anyone he'd cheated would get back *four times* as much.

Because he'd been saved, Zaccheus could do good, selfless things. If you know Jesus, you can too! When you do wrong, admit it and make things right. God will be pleased—and the world will become just a little bit better.

BIBLE ADVENTURE PRAYER STARTER

Jesus, thank You for saving Zaccheus—
and for saving me! Help me to
make my world a better place.

BIBLE ADVENTURE MEMORY VERSE

Tell your sins to each other. And pray
for each other so you may be healed.
JAMES 5:16

JUDAS ISCARIOT:
THE TERRIBLE, HORRIBLE, NO GOOD ADVENTURE

Judas Iscariot was one of the twelve followers. He went to the head religious leaders of the Jews to talk about how he might hand Jesus over to them.

MARK 14:10

Adventures are usually happy, memorable things. But they can also be dangerous—like Judas Iscariot's terrible, horrible, no good adventure.

Judas Iscariot was one of Jesus' twelve disciples. He served with the famous ones like Peter and John, and another guy named Judas. "Iscariot" might have indicated this Judas' hometown.

Since Jesus is God, He knows everything. He knew Judas would turn against Him for money. But He still chose Judas as a disciple. It's hard for us to understand, but the awful betrayal was part of God's plan to save people.

The other disciples thought Judas was okay. They even trusted him to carry their money. Only after his sin against Jesus did the others realize who Judas really was. One called him a thief: "He carried the bag of money and would steal some of it for himself" (John 12:6).

Perhaps greed made Judas lead angry Jewish leaders to Jesus for thirty silver coins. Or maybe money wasn't the reason. Judas might have been disappointed in Jesus. Many thought the Messiah should be a powerful king who freed Israel from Roman rule. But Jesus' kingdom—at least at that time—was purely spiritual.

Either way, Judas turned against Jesus. As a disciple, he'd had every opportunity to learn from Jesus. He should have known who Jesus was and why He came to earth—to save people from sin. But Judas never took advantage of his great privilege. What should have been an incredible adventure of knowing the Lord turned into a disaster. After betraying Jesus, Judas was so sorry that he killed himself.

Judas knew *about* Jesus but didn't really know Him. May we never make that mistake! Though we can't see or hear Jesus the way Judas could, we can read the Bible and pray and listen to His Holy Spirit. We have the opportunity to love Jesus as our best friend—so let's take advantage of it every day.

BIBLE ADVENTURE PRAYER STARTER

Jesus, help me to know and love You,
every day and in every way.

BIBLE ADVENTURE MEMORY VERSE

*I was made right with God by faith
in Christ. I want to know Him.*
PHILIPPIANS 3:9–10

ESAU:
OFFERING FORGIVENESS

Jacob went before them. He bowed to the ground seven times, until he came near his brother. But Esau ran to meet him and put his arms around him and kissed him. And they cried.

GENESIS 33:3–4

~~~~~~~~~~

Esau wanted to kill his slightly younger brother. That's no exaggeration. He was planning to *murder* Jacob.

Why was Esau so mad? Because sneaky Jacob had cheated him—twice.

The boys were twins, but not identical. Esau was born first, red and hairy, with Jacob's hand holding on to his heel! As they grew up, their differences grew too. Esau loved hunting outdoors. Jacob liked to stay at home. He only hunted for ways to mess with Esau.

One day Jacob was cooking. Esau came back from hunting super hungry. So he asked for some stew. Jacob suggested a trade: one bowlful for Esau's birthright. That was a special gift for a firstborn son. When their father, Isaac, died, Esau would get most of the money and leadership of the family. On this day, because he thought he was starving, he foolishly agreed to give Jacob the birthright.

Later, when Isaac was dying, Jacob also stole

Esau's blessing! Old, blind Isaac was ready to share his blessings with his boys. Jacob dressed in Esau's rough, outdoor clothes, pretending to be his older brother. Isaac was confused—this son sounded like Jacob but felt and smelled like Esau. In the end, he promised good things to his dishonest younger son. When Esau found out, he was furious. "The days when I will have sorrow for the loss of my father are soon," he thought. "Then I will kill my brother Jacob" (Genesis 27:41).

Jacob ran away from home to protect himself. Years later he heard that Esau was coming to meet him—with an army of four hundred men. Jacob was terrified. But when Esau finally saw Jacob, he ran to give him a hug. The brothers kissed and cried. Esau had forgiven his brother.

Forgiveness turns enemies into friends. It sets you free to pursue great new adventures.

BIBLE ADVENTURE PRAYER STARTER

Heavenly Father, I don't want to carry around anger and hatred. Help me to forgive!

BIBLE ADVENTURE MEMORY VERSE

You must be kind to each other. Think of the other person. Forgive other people just as God forgave you because of Christ's death on the cross.
EPHESIANS 4:32

JESUS' BROTHERS:
WORK IN PROGRESS

The brothers of Jesus said to Him, "Leave here and go to the country of Judea. Let Your followers there see the things You do. . . . Since You are doing such things, show Yourself to the world." Not even His brothers were putting their trust in Him.
JOHN 7:3–5

Businesses often use the phrase "work in progress." It describes a job somewhere between the idea stage and the final product. When you think about it, every Christian is a work in progress, somewhere between first meeting Jesus and the perfection of heaven.

Jesus is patient with us during that time. He knows we'll need to learn and grow—and that we'll make mistakes along the way. We'll be a lot like His own brothers.

Did you know Jesus had brothers? There were four—James, Joseph, Simon, and Judas. He also had at least three sisters. Someone asks in Matthew 13:56, "Are not all His sisters here?" That "all" means there were more than two.

Jesus was Mary's first child, so His siblings were all younger. Imagine how hard it would be to have a *perfect* older brother. Jesus never did a single bad thing. It seems His brothers were a little frustrated.

As young men, Jesus' brothers criticized Him. He'd been preaching in public, but the Jewish leaders wanted to kill Him. Jesus was being careful, but His brothers demanded, "Show Yourself to the world." The apostle John said Jesus' brothers didn't even believe in Him.

But that was then. Over time they began to realize who their older brother was—the Son of God, the Savior. After Jesus died, was buried, came back to life, and rose up to heaven, the "work in progress" took a big jump forward. His brothers learned and grew. James became a church leader and wrote a book of the Bible. Judas also wrote a Bible book: Jude.

The Christian life is a process. It's okay if you're not perfect yet. Keep reading your Bible, keep praying, keep doing what God says—and one day your work in progress will be complete.

BIBLE ADVENTURE PRAYER STARTER

Lord Jesus, I believe in You. Please keep me moving forward toward perfection.

BIBLE ADVENTURE MEMORY VERSE

We are to hold to the truth with love in our hearts. We are to grow up and be more like Christ.
EPHESIANS 4:15

ELIJAH:
REMEMBER WHAT GOD HAS DONE

*He came to a cave, and stayed there. The
word of the Lord came to him, and said,
"What are you doing here, Elijah?"*
1 KINGS 19:9

~~~~~~~~~~

Heroic Bible men and women had some incredible adventures. But don't think they were superhuman—they were a lot like us. We remember them simply because they obeyed when God told them to do something. And the results were amazing!

You remember Elijah, right? He was a prophet of the one true God, who stood up against 450 prophets of the false god Baal. When Elijah prayed for fire to fall on a sacrifice, God sent it—big time. Everyone could see that God was real and Baal was a fake.

The New Testament writer James (who was probably a brother of Jesus) wrote that "Elijah was a man as we are" (James 5:17). He wasn't super special on his own—Elijah just let God use him. But after God showed such extraordinary power through Elijah, the prophet seemed to forget all about it.

An evil queen named Jezebel worshipped Baal. She was mad that Elijah had embarrassed her fake god. And Jezebel was really angry that Elijah had commanded the people to kill Baal's 450 prophets.

The queen sent a message to Elijah, saying, "So may the gods do to me and even more, if I do not make your life as the life of one of them by this time tomorrow" (1 Kings 19:2). That's a lot of words just to say, "I promise to kill *you*, Elijah."

Suddenly Elijah was afraid. He jumped up and ran for his life into the desert. There, sitting under a tree, he asked *God* to kill him.

Of course, God didn't answer that prayer. He just gently reminded Elijah that He was the same powerful God who had just recently whipped Baal.

Elijah needed to remember what God had done. That's a good lesson for us too. We've seen God do amazing things before. So when scary times come, let's bring those things to mind. We can expect God to do great things again!

BIBLE ADVENTURE PRAYER STARTER

Lord, help me to remember Your great works—and trust You when things get scary.

BIBLE ADVENTURE MEMORY VERSE

Let the joy of Your saving power return to me. And give me a willing spirit to obey you.
PSALM 51:12

JOSEPH OF ARIMATHEA:
GROWING BOLD

*Joseph, who was from the city of Arimathea,
was an important man in the court.
He was looking for the holy nation of God.
Without being afraid, he went to Pilate
and asked for the body of Jesus.*

MARK 15:43

~~~~~~~~~~~~~~~

Scripture mentions more than ten men named
Joseph. One famous Joseph was the husband
of Mary, Jesus' mother. Another Joseph, "of Arimathea," entered Jesus' story toward the end of
His life on earth. He's a great example of growing
bold as a believer.

Joseph was rich and important. He was a Jewish
leader, part of a court called the Sanhedrin (*san-
HEE-drin*). Most of them hated Jesus and wanted
Him to go away. Many wanted to kill Him! But
Joseph had heard and believed Jesus' teaching.
He followed Jesus, but secretly—because he "was
afraid of the Jews" (John 19:38).

We don't know how long Joseph followed Jesus. But after the other leaders finally got what they
wanted—Jesus killed on a cross—Joseph grew bold
in his faith. He went to Pilate, the Roman governor,
and asked for Jesus' body. Joseph wanted to give
his Lord a proper burial.

Joseph knew that the other leaders had lied about Jesus. He knew Jesus had been killed unfairly. Joseph "was a good man and one who did right," a man who "did not agree with what the court did" (Luke 23:50–51).

Maybe Jesus' behavior had given Joseph courage. He had seen Jesus take the court's insults without fighting back. Joseph might even have heard Jesus' prayer from the cross: "Father, forgive them. They do not know what they are doing" (Luke 23:34). Maybe Joseph thought, *If Jesus can face death like that for me, I can honor Him boldly by burying His body!* So Joseph, with the help of Nicodemus, took Jesus' body off the cross and put it in his own unused tomb.

The more we know about Jesus, the more we'll love Him. The more we love Him, the bolder we'll be in standing up for Him. To be like Joseph, read your Bible and pray every day. You'll grow—in boldness!

BIBLE ADVENTURE PRAYER STARTER

Jesus, I want to honor You boldly. Let me know You and love You and speak up for You!

BIBLE ADVENTURE MEMORY VERSE

We speak without fear because our trust is in Christ.
2 Corinthians 3:12

PETER:
REACH OUT!

Peter went up on the roof to pray. He became very hungry and wanted something to eat. While they were getting food ready to eat, he saw in a dream things God wanted him to see. He saw heaven open up and something like a large linen cloth being let down to earth by the four corners. On the cloth were all kinds of four-footed animals and snakes of the earth and birds of the sky. A voice came to him, "Get up, Peter, kill something and eat it."
ACTS 10:9–13

~~~~~~~~~~~~~~~~

Ever had a strange dream? Peter sure did. But God used that dream to send an important message.

Long before Peter's time, God told His people they should not eat certain foods. The Israelites should avoid meat from pigs, rabbits, lizards, and many kinds of birds. Peter always followed those rules. So when a voice in his dream told him to kill and eat an "unclean" animal, he said no.

But the voice answered, "What God has made clean you must not say is unclean" (Acts 10:15). This happened three times in Peter's dream before the sheet and animals went back up to heaven.

Peter woke up wondering about the dream. Right then, God's Spirit told Peter that three men had come to see him. They were servants of a Roman army commander named Cornelius. (You'll learn more about him shortly.)

Normally, Jewish people did not visit or eat meals with non-Jewish people, called "Gentiles." The Romans were Gentiles. But Peter quickly understood that his dream wasn't really about animals—it was about *people*. God was saying that Peter should never avoid other people just because they had a different background or nationality. So Peter quickly invited the visitors in for the night. The next day he went to the house of Cornelius, where he shared the good news about Jesus.

Peter's dream was about reaching out—to anyone you meet who needs to know Jesus. Because *everyone* needs Jesus, you'll have lots of new friends to make.

BIBLE ADVENTURE PRAYER STARTER

Heavenly Father, I'm glad that Jesus came for all people. Give me courage to share His good news with everyone.

BIBLE ADVENTURE MEMORY VERSE

Men become right with God by putting their trust in Jesus Christ. God will accept men if they come this way. All men are the same to God.
ROMANS 3:22

CORNELIUS:
JOIN IN!

Cornelius. . .was a captain of an Italian group of the army. He and his family were good people and honored God. He gave much money to the people and prayed always to God.
ACTS 10:1-2

~~~~~~~~~~~~~~~~

When Jesus lived on earth, His nation was controlled by the Roman Empire. Rome sent soldiers to Israel to make sure the people behaved. Many people in Israel hated being under Rome's power. But they could do little to change it.

Jesus was crucified because some of His own people, the Jews, hated Him. But it was Roman soldiers who actually put Jesus on the cross. Do you remember what Jesus prayed as they nailed Him to the wood? "Father, forgive them. They do not know what they are doing" (Luke 23:34).

Soldiers can be rough guys—they have to be to fight in wars. But some soldiers are kind and generous and helpful, like Cornelius. After Jesus had gone back to heaven and His church was growing in Israel, this man—a Roman "centurion"—did much good for the Jewish people. Cornelius believed in God and prayed regularly. He was generous to his Jewish neighbors. Cornelius was such a good man that an angel came to him, saying, "God has heard your prayers and remembered your gifts of love.

You must send to Joppa and ask Simon Peter to come here" (Acts 10:31–32).

Why should Cornelius invite Peter to his home? So this Roman soldier could hear the *whole* story of God—that Cornelius could join God's family by knowing and following Jesus.

When Peter arrived, he told Cornelius and his relatives about Jesus. They all believed, received the Holy Spirit, and were baptized. Suddenly Jesus' church now had Gentile members from Europe. Christianity was spreading out because Cornelius had joined in. Through Cornelius we see that Gentiles are just as welcome in God's family as Jews.

BIBLE ADVENTURE PRAYER STARTER

God, it's great to be part of Your family. I thank You for offering salvation to everyone!

BIBLE ADVENTURE MEMORY VERSE

There is no difference between the Jews and the people who are not Jews. They are all the same to the Lord. . . . He gives of His greatness to all who call on Him for help.
ROMANS 10:12

MIRIAM:
SPEAK UP

The daughter of Pharaoh came to wash herself in the Nile. Her young women walked beside the Nile. She saw the basket in the tall grass and sent the woman who served her to get it. She opened it and saw the child. The boy was crying. She had pity on him and said, "This is one of the Hebrews' children." Then his sister said to Pharaoh's daughter, "Should I go and call a nurse from the Hebrew women to nurse the child for you?"

EXODUS 2:5-7

~~~~~~~~~~~

Miriam was the oldest child in her family. She and her brothers became leaders among the Hebrew people. Miriam became a prophetess—a woman who spoke for God among the Israelites. Her younger brother Aaron became Israel's first high priest. And baby brother Moses grew up to lead the whole nation for many years.

But when they were all just kids, Miriam showed great courage.

She might have been only six or eight or ten when Moses was born. The family lived in Egypt, where evil Pharaoh had ordered every Israelite baby boy thrown into the Nile River. Moses' mom kept him alive for three months. But when she knew she could no longer hide him, she put him in the river in a floating basket.

Miriam kept watch over her brother. She was by the river's edge when Pharaoh's daughter came to the water to bathe. She discovered the crying baby and felt sorry for him.

And then Miriam spoke up: "Should I go and call a nurse from the Hebrew women to nurse the child for you?" This little girl encouraged the king's daughter to save Moses' life. And Pharaoh's daughter did! Miriam was told to find someone, and she quickly brought her own mother. Moses' mom was able to care for him—and get paid for it.

All because Miriam spoke up. Maybe someday *you'll* have a chance to speak up too—to defend someone who is being bullied, to make peace when people are fighting, to tell someone how Jesus saves. Ask God now for the courage you'll need then. You never know when that moment will happen.

BIBLE ADVENTURE PRAYER STARTER

Lord God, please use my voice to accomplish good things. Help me to speak up when the moment is right.

BIBLE ADVENTURE MEMORY VERSE

Say what is good. Your words should help others grow as Christians.
EPHESIANS 4:29

NEHEMIAH:
TAKING CHARGE

*They said to me, "The Jews who are left who
have returned to the land from Babylon are in
much trouble and shame. The wall of Jerusalem
is broken down and its gates are destroyed by
fire." When I heard this, I sat down and cried
and was filled with sorrow for days. I did not
eat, and I prayed to the God of heaven.*
NEHEMIAH 1:3–4

~~~~~~~~~~~~~~~

When we see a problem, we often think, *Someone
should do something about that!* Ever stop to think
that that "someone" might be you?

When Nehemiah learned that Jerusalem's walls
needed repairs, the first thing he did was pray. Then
he quickly got permission to go to Jerusalem and
start working!

Enemy armies had destroyed Jerusalem more
than a hundred years earlier. The soldiers took
many Jewish people prisoner, hauling them off to
Babylon. Nehemiah had been born in Babylon, but
as a Jewish man, he loved Jerusalem. He wanted
to honor God by rebuilding the city's broken-down
walls.

Jerusalem was now controlled by Persia, and
Nehemiah worked for the king, Artaxerxes. The king
gave Nehemiah everything he asked for—time off,
protection for the journey, and building supplies.

Nehemiah knew exactly why Artaxerxes was so generous—"because the good hand of my God was upon me" (Nehemiah 2:8).

Nehemiah went to Jerusalem and did a nighttime inspection of the ruined walls. Then he gathered the city leaders and urged them to help him rebuild. They agreed, and groups of people started working on different sections.

Enemies of the Jews tried to stop the work. Sometimes they just said mean things. But when they threatened to kill the builders, the Jews started working with one hand and carrying a weapon in the other!

None of this could have happened without Nehemiah's leadership. He saw a need, asked God for help, and got to work. You can do that too. Don't just say, "Someone should do something." Ask God, "What can I do?"

(In case you're curious, those walls that had been broken down for more than a hundred years were fixed in fifty-two days.)

BIBLE ADVENTURE PRAYER STARTER

Lord, I'd like to be like Nehemiah. When I see something that needs to be done, help me to take charge and do it!

BIBLE ADVENTURE MEMORY VERSE

"The God of heaven will make it go well for us."
NEHEMIAH 2:20

JOSEPH, HUSBAND OF MARY:
ADVENTURES IN PROTECTION

Joseph was her promised husband. He was a good man and did not want to make it hard for Mary in front of people. He thought it would be good to break the promised marriage without people knowing it.

MATTHEW 1:19

~~~~~~~~~~

Some adventurous kids grow up to be soldiers, firefighters, or police officers. For many, the danger of protecting others is exciting.

A man named Joseph was a great protector. We don't know if he was excited, but there certainly was danger. You know Joseph as the husband of Mary, Jesus' mother. Joseph served as an earthly dad to Jesus, though God was His real Father.

A carpenter in the town of Nazareth, Joseph was "espoused"—like an engagement—to Mary. But before they got married, she became pregnant, a big problem for a girl in that time and place. Joseph knew the baby wasn't his, and he could have made life hard for Mary. But he was good and kind, so he decided to quietly end their engagement. Joseph protected Mary even when it seemed like she'd done something wrong.

Then an angel spoke to Joseph in a dream,

telling him that Mary's baby was actually the Son of God! Joseph believed the angel, married Mary, and became "dad" to Jesus a few months later.

Soon Mary and Jesus both needed Joseph's protection. The angel spoke to Joseph in another dream: "Take the young Child and His mother to the country of Egypt. . . . Stay there until you hear from Me. Herod is going to look for the young Child to kill Him" (Matthew 2:13). Immediately Joseph got his family ready and left for Egypt. He didn't return to his own country until the angel told him King Herod was dead.

It's good to protect others. If you notice a toddler heading toward the street, stop him. If you see a girl being bullied at school, stand up for her. If you meet people who don't know Jesus, tell them the good news of salvation—that will protect them for all eternity! God is pleased when you look out for the well-being of others.

BIBLE ADVENTURE PRAYER STARTER

Lord, give me courage to protect and defend others. I want to be good and kind like Joseph.

BIBLE ADVENTURE MEMORY VERSE

Stand up for the rights of those who are suffering and in need.
PROVERBS 31:9

CALEB:
SPY WITH A DIFFERENT SPIRIT

Caleb told the people in front of Moses to be quiet. And he said, "Let us go up at once and take the land. For we are well able to take it in battle."
NUMBERS 13:30

~~~~~~~~~~~

Sometimes before a battle, an army sends spies into enemy territory. They might sneak around in the dark. They might dress like the enemy so nobody realizes they're from the other side. Spies want to learn what their enemies are doing, how strong they are, and how they can be defeated.

Just before God's people entered their promised land, twelve men went to spy on Canaan. Moses chose one from each tribe of Israel, telling them, "See what the land is like. See if the people who live in it are strong or weak, and if they are few or many. Find out if the land they live in is good or bad" (Numbers 13:18–19).

God called Canaan "a land flowing with milk and honey" (Exodus 3:8)—a good place, full of good things. The twelve men who saw Canaan found that God's words were true. (No surprise—God's words are *always* true!)

But the spies also saw very large people and strong cities. Ten spies gave a bad report: "We are not able to go against the people. They are too strong for us" (Numbers 13:31). Those spies felt like grasshoppers compared to Canaan's giants.

Joshua and Caleb, though, trusted God. Caleb said, "Let us go up at once and take the land. For we are well able to take it in battle."

He wasn't boasting. Caleb knew that since God had promised the land, God would give it to Israel. "Do not be afraid of the people of the land," he said. "They have no way to keep safe, and the Lord is with us" (Numbers 14:9).

Sadly, the Israelites listened to the fearful spies. But God paid attention to Caleb, rewarding him for his faith. God said, "My servant Caleb has had a different spirit and has followed Me in every way" (Numbers 14:24).

That's something you can do too!

▶ BIBLE ADVENTURE PRAYER STARTER ◀

Lord, help me to follow You in everything. I want a different spirit from the rest of the world.

▶ BIBLE ADVENTURE MEMORY VERSE ◀

Stand true to the Lord. Keep on acting like men and be strong.
1 CORINTHIANS 16:13

GIDEON:
LESS IS MORE

*Gideon sent all the other men of Israel to
their tents. He kept only the 300 men.*
JUDGES 7:8

~~~~~~~~

Have you ever heard someone say, "Less is more"?
It's a way of looking at choices. For example, if you
do less spending, you end up with more money.

An Old Testament character named Gideon
learned that fewer *soldiers* meant more *God*—and
a miracle victory over a huge enemy army.

Gideon was an Israelite "judge." Judges were
leaders God chose to rescue His people. In Gideon's
time, the powerful Midianites marched through Israel
destroying the people's grain and sheep and cows.

God's angel told Gideon to save Israel. Gideon
didn't think he could. "How can I save Israel?" he
asked. "My family is the least in Manasseh. And
I am the youngest in my father's house" (Judges
6:15). But God made the same promise He makes
to everyone who follows Him: "I will be with you"
(verse 16). So Gideon called up an army of thirty-two
thousand men.

God said that was too many! He didn't want
people to say, "Our own power has saved us"
(Judges 7:2). So God told Gideon to send soldiers
home if they were afraid of fighting. Twenty-two
thousand left.

Now there were ten thousand soldiers, but God said that was still too many. So He had Gideon take them to the river for a drink. Most of them lapped up water like dogs. Only three hundred drank from their cupped hands—and they would be Gideon's entire army.

The "battle" happened at night. Gideon gave each soldier a trumpet and a burning torch covered by a clay pot. As the enemy slept in their tents, Gideon's men blasted their horns and smashed their pots. The noise woke the Midianites, and the light from the torches hurt their eyes. Gideon's soldiers shouted, "A sword for the Lord and for Gideon!" (Judges 7:20) and the Midianites were so confused that they fought against each other!

God plus three hundred soldiers is a winning army. God plus one person—*you*—can accomplish anything He wants. Just work with Him.

BIBLE ADVENTURE PRAYER STARTER

Powerful God, I want to work with You. "Less is more" when You're the one I love most.

BIBLE ADVENTURE MEMORY VERSE

*"Do not fear, for I am with you.
Do not be afraid, for I am your God."*
ISAIAH 41:10

DEBORAH:
UNEXPECTED ADVENTURE

Barak said to her, "I will go if you go with me.
But if you do not go with me, I will not go."
And she said, "For sure I will go with you."
JUDGES 4:8–9

God made men and women to be different. They often think differently. They have different body parts. Usually, men are physically stronger and do more dangerous jobs. But women can be just as bold and adventurous in their own way.

Like Gideon, Deborah was a judge of Israel. Out of more than a dozen judges, she was the only woman. Sometimes Deborah was more like the judges we see today—people who decide the law in a courtroom. The Bible says, "The people of Israel came to her to find out what was right or wrong" (Judges 4:5).

One time, though, Deborah was like a male judge of the Bible—a military leader who rescued the people from their enemies. At first, Deborah just went to Israel's army commander, Barak, to give him a message from God: "The Lord, the God of Israel, says, 'Go to Mount Tabor. Take with you 10,000 men. . . . I will have Sisera, the head of Jabin's army, meet you at the river Kishon. He will have his war-wagons and his many soldiers with him. But I will give him into your hand' " (Judges 4:6–7).

For some reason, Barak didn't want to lead by himself. He said he would only go if Deborah went with him—and she did. This adventurous lady rode into battle with thousands of male soldiers. As promised, God gave the Israelites success. They wiped out Sisera's army with its nine hundred iron chariots. All because Deborah was willing to do something most people didn't expect.

Every day *we* can do something unexpected. We can do more than we're asked to do on a job. We can show kindness to a stranger. We can stand up for the unpopular. These "adventures" may seem small—but they might just point others to our great God.

BIBLE ADVENTURE PRAYER STARTER

Lord, I want others to know You. Help me to obey You boldly and then tell people why!

BIBLE ADVENTURE MEMORY VERSE

"Let your light shine in front of men. Then they will see the good things you do and will honor your Father Who is in heaven."
MATTHEW 5:16

SHADRACH, MESHACH, AND ABED-NEGO:
STANDING TALL TOGETHER

Nebuchadnezzar said to them, "Is it true, Shadrach, Meshach and Abed-nego, that you do not serve my gods or worship the object of gold that I have set up? Now if you are ready to get down on your knees and worship the object I have made. . .very well. But if you will not worship, you will be thrown at once into the fire. And what god is able to save you from my hands?"
DANIEL 3:14-15

~~~~~~~~~~

These guys are always together in the Bible. They were probably together a lot in life too.

Imagine being young, smart, and good looking. (You probably don't need to imagine that!) Now imagine that an enemy nation has taken over your country—and because you're young, smart, and good looking, the invading king wants you to serve him. That's what happened to these Jewish friends.

They were taken to Babylon to work for the powerful, scary King Nebuchadnezzar. He had destroyed their homeland. Then one of his officials changed their names. Originally called Hananiah, Mishael, and Azariah—names that all said good things about God—they soon sounded like any other Babylonian. But they didn't act like Babylonians.

The king got some crazy idea to set up a huge

golden statue and make everyone bow down and worship it. Then he commanded anyone who disobeyed to be thrown into a blazing furnace. It might have been a place where bricks were baked or iron ore melted.

But you know what happened next: In the huge crowd of people bowing before that silly idol, three guys stood tall. Shadrach, Meshach, and Abed-nego told Nebuchadnezzar no. He'd tried to separate them from God, but they stuck together in their faith. They trusted God more than they feared Nebuchadnezzar. And that was the right choice: though the king did throw them into the fire, God brought them through without the slightest harm.

Good friends can do great things when they stand together for God.

BIBLE ADVENTURE PRAYER STARTER

Lord God, please give me friends like Shadrach, Meshach, and Abed-nego. I want to be around people who encourage me to stand tall for You.

BIBLE ADVENTURE MEMORY VERSE

One man is able to have power over him who is alone, but two can stand against him. It is not easy to break a rope made of three strings.
ECCLESIASTES 4:12

SAMSON:
STRONG BODY, WEAK SPIRIT

*Samson said, "Let me die with the Philistines!"
Then he pushed with all his strength
so that the building fell on the leaders
and all the people in it. He killed more
at his death than he killed in his life.*

JUDGES 16:30

~~~~~~~~~

Talk about a warrior! Samson once killed a thousand enemy soldiers all by himself, using a donkey's jawbone as a weapon. It's hard to imagine that kind of power.

Samson's incredible strength came straight from God. A miracle baby, Samson was born to a couple who'd been unable to have kids. God's angel said this special son would grow up to rescue Israel from its enemies.

The angel had a special rule for Samson: no haircuts! As his hair grew, so did his strength.

Samson was a "judge," or deliverer, of Israel. When the people sinned, God allowed other nations to punish them. When the people cried out, God sent judges to rescue them. The Israelites realized they were wrong and turned back to God—for a while. Sadly, God sent many judges because the people often sinned.

Even Samson had trouble with that. He was strong in body but weak in spirit, with very little self-control. He even fell in love with Philistine women! He should have run away. When he didn't, there was big trouble.

One woman, Delilah, tricked Samson into telling the secret of his strength. When he admitted it was his hair, know what she did? Yep. She shaved it all off as he slept! Samson lost his strength and became a prisoner.

In jail, Samson was probably sorry for how foolish he'd been. But his hair started growing back. One day the Philistines brought Samson to the temple of their false god to make fun of him. That's when God used Samson one last time. Strong again in the Lord's strength, he pushed on the pillars of the building. It fell down and killed everyone—including Samson.

What a sad story. Samson did many good things, but his selfishness really messed him up. Whatever special abilities God gives you, be sure you use them for *Him*. Then you'll never look back with sorrow.

BIBLE ADVENTURE PRAYER STARTER

Lord God, help me always to obey You and use my talents for Your glory.

BIBLE ADVENTURE MEMORY VERSE

"It is better to obey than to give gifts."
1 SAMUEL 15:22

HEZEKIAH:
GO STRAIGHT TO GOD

Hezekiah took the letter from the hand of the men from Assyria, and read it. Then he went up to the house of the Lord, and spread the letter out before the Lord. Hezekiah prayed to the Lord, saying. . . "O Lord our God, I beg You to save us from his power."
2 KINGS 19:14–15, 19

To understand Hezekiah's story, you need to know some history.

Long before Hezekiah, God had chosen Abraham to start a special nation called Israel. God would be Israel's king. One day this nation would bless everyone on earth by producing the Messiah, Jesus, who saves people from their sins.

But God's people often disobeyed Him. They didn't want to follow His rules. They wanted a king like every other nation. God warned them that a human king could be bad for them, but He gave them what they wanted. Israel's first king was Saul, followed by David (the best), and David's son Solomon. When Solomon's son Rehoboam took over, he was mean and foolish. Many in northern Israel broke away and made a smaller nation, still called Israel. Rehoboam led a smaller nation in the south called Judah.

Every king in Israel's history was bad. Some of Judah's kings were bad too, but Hezekiah was very good. The Bible says he "trusted in the Lord, the God of Israel. There was no one like him among all the kings of Judah before him or after him" (2 Kings 18:5).

Because Israel and its kings were so sinful, God sent a nation called Assyria to destroy them. But when Assyria came against Judah, Hezekiah knew exactly what to do. He took the enemy's threatening letter and laid it out before God. Then Hezekiah asked God to save Judah—which God did in an amazing way. He sent an angel who killed 185,000 Assyrian soldiers in the night!

Hezekiah set a great example for you. When you have a big, tough problem, go straight to God. He knows exactly what you need, and He's always ready to help.

BIBLE ADVENTURE PRAYER STARTER

Heavenly Father, there are lots of scary people and things in my world. You know exactly how to help me. Please do!

BIBLE ADVENTURE MEMORY VERSE

God is our safe place and our strength. He is always our help when we are in trouble.
PSALM 46:1

JOSIAH:
KID KING

Before Josiah there was no king like him who turned to the Lord with all his heart and soul and strength, obeying all the Law of Moses. And no one like him came after him.
2 Kings 23:25

~~~~~~~~~~~~~~~~~

Josiah was another very good king of Judah. His story is amazing when you realize that his father and grandfather were both horrible kings. . .and that Josiah was only eight years old when he began to rule!

Josiah's grandfather was Manasseh, a violent idol worshipper who reigned fifty-five long years. When Manasseh died, his wicked son Amon became king. Amon was so bad that his servants killed him after two years. The people of Judah knew that was wrong, so they killed the men who killed Amon. Then they made Amon's young son, Josiah, king.

At age sixteen, Josiah "began to look for the God of his father [or ancestor] David" (2 Chronicles 34:3). By the time he was twenty, he was tearing down idols and altars to false gods in Judah. When he was twenty-six, Josiah started repairing God's temple, which Manasseh and Amon never cared about. During the work, someone found the book of God's law and brought it to the king.

Josiah knew *about* God. But when he learned

exactly what God's law said, he was upset. "The Lord is very angry with us," Josiah said, "because our fathers have not listened to the words of this book. They have not done all that is written for us to do" (2 Kings 22:13).

God said Josiah's response was good. "When you heard this, you were sorry in your heart," the Lord said. "You have torn your clothes and cried before Me, and I have heard you" (2 Kings 22:19). Josiah served God well, always urging the people of Judah to do right.

Josiah proves two important things. First, even very young people can serve God. And second, it doesn't matter what kind of family you come from. Josiah's dad and grandpa were evil men, but he became one of Judah's godliest kings.

Your relationship with God is totally up to you.

▶ BIBLE ADVENTURE PRAYER STARTER ◀

Lord, I'm young—but I can still serve You with all my heart. Help me to be bold and adventurous like Josiah!

▶ BIBLE ADVENTURE MEMORY VERSE ◀

How can a young man keep his way pure? By living by Your Word.
PSALM 119:9

PAUL:
A PREVIEW OF HEAVEN!

I have to talk about myself, even if it does no good. But I will keep on telling about some things I saw in a special dream and that which the Lord has shown me. I know a man who belongs to Christ. Fourteen years ago he was taken up to the highest heaven. . . . The things God showed me were so great. But to keep me from being too full of pride because of seeing these things, I have been given trouble in my body. It was sent from Satan to hurt me. It keeps me from being proud.

2 CORINTHIANS 12:1–2, 7

People who follow Jesus on earth expect to be with Him in heaven someday. The Bible tells us a few things about heaven but leaves a lot of details unsaid. So it's hard to imagine exactly what God's home is like.

The apostle Paul didn't have to imagine. While he was still alive on earth, God actually took him on a tour of heaven! There Paul learned things that "no man is allowed to tell" (2 Corinthians 12:4). How cool is that?

Maybe just a little too cool. Paul admitted that his amazing trip might make him proud. Hey, who else gets to visit heaven and then come back to earth? So God sent Paul "trouble in [his] body" (verse 7). That would keep the apostle humble and remind him to use his vision only to help other people.

Our big adventures and exciting accomplishments are great gifts from God Himself. Just never forget those last four words—they're *gifts from God Himself*. Make sure you give Him, rather than yourself, all the credit. Then you'll be like Paul, and your adventures will accomplish great things for everyone.

BIBLE ADVENTURE PRAYER STARTER

Dear Lord, thank You for all the gifts You provide, on this earth and in heaven to come. I want to look forward to eternity with You and bring along as many of my friends and family as possible.

BIBLE ADVENTURE MEMORY VERSE

"No eye has ever seen or no ear has ever heard or no mind has ever thought of the wonderful things God has made ready for those who love Him."
1 CORINTHIANS 2:9

PRISCILLA AND AQUILA:
ADVENTURING TOGETHER

Paul went from the city of Athens and came to the city of Corinth. He met a Jew there named Aquila who was born in the country of Pontus. He had lived in the country of Italy for a short time. His wife Priscilla was with him. Claudius, who was the leader of the country, had told all the Jews to leave Rome. Paul went to see Aquila and Priscilla. They made tents for a living. Paul did the same kind of work so he stayed with them and they worked together.

ACTS 18:1–3

～～～～～～

At some point in life, probably not too far in the future, you'll discover the "opposite sex." Boys find that they like girls, and girls get interested in boys. As you grow older, you'll likely meet someone special and decide to get married. It's a wonderful thing when a husband and wife both love and serve God.

That's how Priscilla and Aquila were. They were Jews who had heard about and believed in Jesus. For a while, they lived in the huge city of Rome, but the Roman emperor demanded that all the Jews leave. So Priscilla and Aquila ended up in Corinth, about six hundred miles to the east, where they met the apostle Paul.

Before long, Paul and this Christian couple were working together. They made money by sewing tents to sell. And they shared the gospel with people wherever they went. One time Priscilla and Aquila stayed in the city of Ephesus after Paul moved on. The powerful preacher Apollos came to town, and Priscilla and Aquila heard him speak. He said a lot of good things about Jesus, but he didn't know everything about salvation. So this wise couple invited Apollos to their home, where they taught him more about the things of God.

Every time you read about Priscilla in the Bible, you also find Aquila. That's one of the great things about marriage—the close bond between a husband and wife. Maybe someday God will give you that blessing too. The faith life is an adventure. . .one that's great to experience *together*.

BIBLE ADVENTURE PRAYER STARTER

Lord, if You want me to get married someday, please lead me to the person who's perfect for me. You already know who that is!

BIBLE ADVENTURE MEMORY VERSE

Marriage should be respected by everyone.
HEBREWS 13:4

JOSHUA:
THE SUN STANDS STILL!

Then Joshua spoke to the Lord on the day when the Lord made the Amorites lose the war against the sons of Israel. He said, in the eyes of Israel, "O sun, stand still at Gibeon. O moon, stand still in the valley of Aijalon." So the sun stood still and the moon stopped, until the nation punished those who fought against them.
JOSHUA 10:12–13

~~~~~~~~~~

You probably know that prayer is just talking to God. But there are different kinds of prayer.

Praise is telling God how great He is. *Confession* is admitting to God that you've sinned. *Thanksgiving* is just like it sounds—giving thanks to God for all He is and does.

Then there are *supplications* or *petitions*. These are the prayers that ask God for something. You might "petition" God to give you a friend at school or to heal someone who is sick. Joshua asked God to make the sun stand still in the sky.

Huh?

It's true. Joshua was leading God's people, the Israelites, in a battle against the Amorites. Things were going well for Joshua, since God was helping. But the day was getting short, and Joshua wanted to finish the battle before nighttime. So he prayed one of the craziest prayers you'll ever hear about: "O sun, stand still at Gibeon. O moon, stand still in the valley of Aijalon." If the sun and moon stopped in the sky, Joshua would have enough daylight to complete his job.

And God gave Joshua what he wanted! Whoever wrote the book of Joshua said, "There has been no day like it before or since, when the Lord listened to the voice of a man. For the Lord fought for Israel" (Joshua 10:14).

God doesn't answer every prayer like He answered Joshua's. Even Jesus got a "no" once, when He asked His Father if He could avoid the pain of the cross (see Matthew 26:39, Mark 14:36, and Luke 22:42). But God has the power to do any amazing thing that supports His perfect plans, so why not ask? He may shock you with His "yes"!

BIBLE ADVENTURE PRAYER STARTER

Lord God, I know You can do anything!
Give me the confidence to make
big, important requests of You.

BIBLE ADVENTURE MEMORY VERSE

*The prayer from the heart of a man
right with God has much power.*
JAMES 5:16

MARY, SISTER OF MARTHA:
CLOSE TO JESUS

Many of the Jews who had come to visit Mary and had seen what Jesus had done put their trust in Him.
JOHN 11:45

~~~~~~~~

Do you remember Martha's story? She wanted her sister, Mary, to help out more when Jesus visited. But He said that *Mary* had chosen the better thing—just being close to Him.

The sisters had a brother named Lazarus. You probably know that Jesus brought him back to life! Here is Mary's part in that story:

Lazarus had died four days earlier. Martha heard Jesus was on His way to their town and ran out to see Him. Mary stayed at home with people who'd come to cry over their loss.

Jesus told Martha that He had power over death, and she ran back to tell Mary. Martha whispered to Mary, "The Teacher is here and has sent for you" (John 11:28), so she quickly left the house. The others thought Mary was going to the grave to cry. . .so they followed her.

They soon learned that Mary had gone to see Jesus. Even He was sad and crying. "See how much He loved Lazarus," people said (John 11:36). Jesus *did* love Lazarus, just as He loved Mary and Martha. But Jesus' love was more than simply words and tears—it was action. Soon He was shouting into the tomb, "Lazarus, come out!" (verse 43). And the brother of Mary and Martha, dead for days, was alive again!

Mary saw Lazarus raised to life by the friend she knew as the Son of God. She always enjoyed being with Jesus and learning from Him. Now that closeness was rewarded in an extraordinary way: her beloved brother was back from the dead.

Even in Bible times, that kind of miracle was unusual. But God promises that everyone who follows Jesus will "rise from the dead" to eternal life. When you believe in Jesus' life, death, and resurrection, you can expect a life with Him that goes far beyond—*forever* beyond—the end of this life. Closeness to Jesus begins the ultimate adventure.

BIBLE ADVENTURE PRAYER STARTER

Lord Jesus, keep me close to You—forever!

BIBLE ADVENTURE MEMORY VERSE

Jesus said to her, "I am the One Who raises the dead and gives them life. Anyone who puts his trust in Me will live again, even if he dies."
JOHN 11:25

LEGION:
AN INCREDIBLE CHANGE

*The man spoke with a loud voice and said,
"What do You want with me, Jesus, Son
of the Most High God? I ask You, in the
name of God, do not hurt me!" At the same
time, Jesus was saying, "Come out of the
man, you demon!" Jesus asked the demon,
"What is your name?" He said, "My name
is Many, for there are many of us."*

MARK 5:7–9

~~~~~~~~

Some Bible stories are a little creepy. Like this one about a demon-possessed man.

Demons are evil spirit beings who follow and serve Satan. In Bible times, they sometimes "possessed" people. That means they would live inside those people, taking over their mind and speech and actions. Demon-possessed people were miserable. They often tried to hurt themselves.

This troubled man called himself "Many" because there were so many demons inside him. Some Bible translations call him "Legion," after a unit in the Roman army. A legion contained five thousand men, so imagine how this poor guy must have felt!

That is, until Jesus showed up.

The demons knew that Jesus could destroy them. They begged Him not to send them away forever. Jesus actually agreed with their request to go into some nearby animals. Two thousand pigs went crazy, rushing down a hill and into a lake, where they drowned.

Meanwhile, the guy once called Legion was all cleaned up and normal again. He wanted to follow Jesus wherever He went. But Jesus told him, "Go home to your own people. Tell them what great things the Lord has done for you" (Mark 5:19). He did, and many people wanted to know more about Jesus.

Hopefully, you'll never have a problem like Legion's. But you'll have troubles of one kind or another—and Jesus will do great things for you too. When He does, show your gratitude by telling others about Him!

BIBLE ADVENTURE PRAYER STARTER

Lord Jesus, You have the power to cast out demons, heal the sick, and even raise people from the dead. You can definitely help me with my problems! When I face trouble, please give me wisdom and peace and hope.

BIBLE ADVENTURE MEMORY VERSE

Praise the Lord, O my soul. And forget none of His acts of kindness. He forgives all my sins. He heals all my diseases.
Psalm 103:2–3

ENOCH:
TELEPORTED

When Enoch had lived sixty-five years,
he became the father of Methuselah.
Enoch walked with God 300 years after
the birth of Methuselah. He had other
sons and daughters. So Enoch lived 365
years. Enoch walked with God, and he
was seen no more, for God took him.
GENESIS 5:21–24

You've probably seen "teleporting" in a movie or TV show: someone steps into a special room in one place, then gets zapped into some other place. How it works is never really explained. But it's fun to imagine, right?

In the Bible, way back in the early part of Genesis, there's a man who basically got teleported to heaven. His name was Enoch.

It was a time when people lived superlong lives. In fact, Enoch's son Methuselah had the longest life of anyone mentioned in the Bible: 969 years! But Enoch was "only" 365 when God swept him up to heaven. Enoch didn't get old and die like everyone else—he was so popular with God that the Lord just took him home one day. The "faith hall of fame" in Hebrews 11 says, "The Holy Writings tell how he pleased God before he was taken up" (verse 5).

What was Enoch's secret? The book of Genesis says he "walked" with God. That means everything he did was centered on God. He listened to God, he obeyed God, he honored God. And he was rewarded by God in a very unusual way.

That's pretty adventurous stuff. Do you think you can "walk with God" today?

BIBLE ADVENTURE PRAYER STARTER

Heavenly Father, I want to please You like Enoch did. I want to walk with You every day and in every way. Please lead and guide me in Your paths, and keep me by Your side. May everything I do be centered on You.

BIBLE ADVENTURE MEMORY VERSE

Happy is the man who does not walk in the way sinful men tell him to, or stand in the path of sinners, or sit with those who laugh at the truth. But he finds joy in the Law of the Lord and thinks about His Law day and night.
PSALM 1:1–2

JOHN THE BAPTIST:
WHEN THINGS GO WRONG

Herod had sent men to take John and put him into prison. He did this because of his wife, Herodias. She had been the wife of his brother Philip. John the Baptist had said to Herod, "It is wrong for you to have your brother's wife." Herodias became angry with him. She wanted to have John the Baptist killed but she could not. . . . Then Herodias found a way.

MARK 6:17–19, 21

What? Someone plotted to kill John the Baptist? Sadly, yes.

Why would the Bible tell us that? Why would a kids' devotional?

Because there are hard, honest truths about life that we all need to learn. Life on this earth doesn't always go smoothly—even for a brave, strong, adventurous guy like John the Baptist. Evil people do evil things, and sometimes what they do affects all of us. That's the bad news.

The good news is that God is always in control. Even if He allows hard things in this life, there's a far better life coming. Really, the eternal life that Jesus offers is perfect.

It's easy to believe that our life on earth is all there is. When we think that way, we look at

John the Baptist and ask, "What went wrong?" The answer is *nothing*. God just took him home to heaven sooner.

When John was killed, he went from being *near* heaven to being *in* heaven. There God probably told him, "You have done well. You are a good and faithful servant. . . . Come and share my joy" (Matthew 25:21). John saw awesome sights, like giant gates of pearl and streets of pure gold (Revelation 21:21). And he enjoyed complete peace and happiness—no arguments, no bullies, no violence or even disappointment (Revelation 21:27).

Now *that's* worth looking forward to. This world will often disappoint us, but heaven never will. That's because heaven is God's home, and nothing ever goes wrong there.

BIBLE ADVENTURE PRAYER STARTER

Lord Jesus, thank You for opening the way to heaven. Remind me that this world is only for a short time. My real home is with You, forever!

BIBLE ADVENTURE MEMORY VERSE

Keep your minds thinking about things in heaven. Do not think about things on the earth.
COLOSSIANS 3:2

SHIPHRAH AND PUAH:
PROTECTING LIFE

Then the king of Egypt spoke to the Hebrew nurses. The name of one was Shiphrah. The name of the other was Puah. He said, "When you are helping the Hebrew women to give birth, and see the baby before the mother does, if it is a son, kill him. But if it is a daughter, let her live." But the nurses feared God. They did not do what the king of Egypt told them. They let the boys live.

EXODUS 1:15–17

God created human life way back in the Garden of Eden. He's given life to everyone since that time. And He wants people to protect life.

Long ago two women did that, and God honored them. He even put their names into scripture so we remember them thousands of years later.

Shiphrah and Puah lived when God's people were slaves in Egypt. At one time, the Egyptian king welcomed the Israelites. But then a new king came along, and he was afraid of the people. He thought there were too many Israelites—they might try to take over his country. So he decided that half of their newborns should be killed!

The king called in some nurses, or "midwives," women who help pregnant ladies give birth. His command to them was, as babies were born, "If it is a son, kill him." Girls could live, though. The king figured they could grow up to work but probably wouldn't fight against him.

Can you imagine how Shiphrah and Puah felt? Their job was to bring life into the world, not destroy it. And they "feared God"—they respected Him as Creator of all things, including life. They chose to disobey the king's evil command.

God was pleased. He protected the women for protecting life and gave them children of their own.

Sometimes we'll face ungodly rules. Sometimes people will urge us to do the wrong thing. At those moments, let's be like Shiphrah and Puah, choosing God's way. Things may get tough, but God will take care of us.

BIBLE ADVENTURE PRAYER STARTER

Heavenly Father, thank You for the life You created and gave to me. Help me to honor Your gift by protecting life.

BIBLE ADVENTURE MEMORY VERSE

"I have put in front of you life and death, the good and the curse. So choose life so you and your children after you may live."
DEUTERONOMY 30:19

JESUS:
SWORDS AND PARADOX

Simon Peter had a sword. He took it and hit a servant who was owned by the head religious leader and cut off his right ear. The servant's name was Malchus. Then Jesus said to Peter, "Put your sword back where it belongs. Am I not to go through what My Father has given Me to go through?"
JOHN 18:10–11

God wants His kids to value life—we learned that from Shiphrah and Puah. But when it comes to our own lives, we shouldn't hold on too tightly. It's a paradox of the Christian faith.

A paradox is something that seems backward but turns out to be true. Jesus taught in paradoxes. One of His big ones was about service: "If anyone wants to be first, he must be last of all. He will be the one to care for all" (Mark 9:35). Another paradox: "If anyone wants to keep his own life safe, he will lose it. If anyone gives up his life because of Me and because of the Good News, he will save it" (Mark 8:35).

Jesus lived out what He taught. He allowed Himself to be arrested in the Garden of Gethsemane because He was going to serve all people of all time by His death on the cross. Jesus didn't try to save His own life—even though Peter wanted to.

When a crowd of men came to capture Jesus, Peter tried to fight back. He had a sword, and he swung it. Since he'd been a fisherman and not a soldier, he wasn't a great swordsman. A man named Malchus ducked, almost out of the way—but Peter's sword slash nicked off his ear.

Jesus' job was to die on the cross, not save His own life. So He told Peter to put the sword away. Then Jesus healed Malchus and allowed Himself to be taken away. He cared much more for other people's lives than His own.

That's a hard lesson to learn, but one that all Christians must. Ask God to help you be more like Jesus.

BIBLE ADVENTURE PRAYER STARTER

Jesus, I want to be more like You—loving and serving everyone, even my enemies. Help me to live out the paradox of following You!

BIBLE ADVENTURE MEMORY VERSE

Most of all, have a true love for each other. Love covers many sins.
1 PETER 4:8

DANIEL:
OBEDIENT IN LITTLE THINGS. . .

Daniel made up his mind that he would not make himself unclean with the king's best food and wine. So he asked the head ruler to allow him not to make himself unclean.

DANIEL 1:8

~~~~~~

Imagine this: Your country has been invaded. Enemy soldiers kidnap you, dragging you off to their capital. You're put into special training, preparing to serve the enemy king. Step one is eating his fancy foods.

Well, at least that food part doesn't sound so bad, right?

Except that your parents had warned you against those foods. You see, God's rules said some foods were okay to eat, and some weren't. The enemy's foods are the wrong kind.

What can you do? You're in an enemy country, under the enemy's control. You have no power to say no.

That's the situation Daniel faced. His nation, Judah, was invaded by Babylon. Daniel was chosen to serve Babylon's king, Nebuchadnezzar. When Daniel was offered the king's food, he knew he couldn't eat it and still please God. So Daniel *did* say no.

He wasn't rude about it. Daniel went to the

Babylonian official in charge, kindly saying, "Test your servants for ten days. Give us only vegetables to eat and water to drink. Then compare how we look with the young men who are eating the king's best food" (Daniel 1:12–13).

God had made the Babylonian official friendly to Daniel. So he agreed to try Daniel's plan. Guess what? After ten days, Daniel and his friends were much healthier than the guys who'd eaten the fancy food!

Daniel went on to become very important in Babylon. God used him to speak truth to that ungodly nation, and to prophesy—tell what would happen in the future—to everyone. Today we still read his prophecies in the Bible's book of Daniel.

That was all possible because Daniel first obeyed God's rules on what to eat. When you're obedient in little things, chances are good you'll do right in the big things. And God will reward your faithfulness.

BIBLE ADVENTURE PRAYER STARTER

Heavenly Father, give me the courage of Daniel to obey You in everything.

BIBLE ADVENTURE MEMORY VERSE

"You are a good servant. You have been faithful in using a little. Now you will be leader over ten cities."
LUKE 19:17

MOSES:
THE BUDDY SYSTEM

*The Lord said to Aaron, "Go to meet Moses
in the desert." So he went and met him
at the mountain of God and kissed him.
Moses told Aaron all the words of the Lord
with which He had sent him. And he told
him about all the special works that the
Lord had told him to do. Then Moses and
Aaron went and gathered together all the
leaders of the people of Israel. Aaron spoke
all the words which the Lord had spoken to
Moses. Then he did all the special works for
the people to see. So the people believed.*

EXODUS 4:27–31

Ever notice how much easier jobs become when
you have help? Raking leaves goes a lot faster with
a friend. It's much easier to rearrange your bedroom
with another person's help. Many things go better
with a friend pitching in.

Friends help us in the adventure of life too.
You might remember that Moses got scared when
God told him to lead the Israelites out of Egypt.
Moses didn't want to march up to the powerful king,
Pharaoh, and say, "You're doing the wrong thing!
Let the people go!" So to help Moses do his job,
God made a plan—let's call it the "buddy system."

God talked to Moses' older brother, Aaron. Aaron went out to meet Moses in the desert. They went *together* to find Pharaoh. When they saw him, they told him *together* what God wanted. And in the end, they got to see—*together*—the Israelites escaping their slavery in Egypt.

Good things happened because Moses had a buddy. If you don't have a caring, helpful friend like that, pray and ask God to give you one. And always be sure to *be* that kind of friend for someone else. Just imagine the good things you might accomplish!

BIBLE ADVENTURE PRAYER STARTER

Father in heaven, You knew that people would need friends. I thank You that Your Son, Jesus, is such a faithful friend to me. Please give me true friends on earth, and help me to be the kind of friend I want others to be to me.

BIBLE ADVENTURE MEMORY VERSE

Help each other in troubles and problems. This is the kind of law Christ asks us to obey.
GALATIANS 6:2

JOSEPH, SON OF JACOB:
DON'T TAKE REVENGE

When Joseph's brothers saw that their father was dead, they said, "It may be now that Joseph will hate us, and pay us in return for all the wrong that we did to him!"
GENESIS 50:15

~~~~~~~~~~~~

Revenge is a kind of payback. If someone hurts you, you hurt them the same way—or worse.

It's natural to want bad people to be punished. But Christians aren't supposed to take revenge. We should love our enemies and pray for them, letting God do the paybacks. That's how Joseph handled his ten brothers who had treated him horribly.

Maybe you know what they did: Jacob's older sons hated their little brother, who was Dad's favorite. So they sold him into slavery. Can you imagine if Joseph ever got a chance for revenge?

Well, he did. But he didn't use it.

Joseph was a good man who honored God through everything. Over time God made things better for Joseph. After many years, he was second in command of Egypt!

One day Joseph's older brothers showed up. They wanted to buy food because there was a shortage—a famine—in their country of Judah. Since Joseph controlled Egypt's food supply, the brothers had to come to him.

What an opportunity! Joseph could have thrown them in jail, whipped them, even killed them. But he didn't do any of that.

Joseph immediately recognized his brothers, though they didn't know who he was. He'd been a helpless teenager the last time they saw him. Now he was a grown man—a powerful national leader.

When Joseph said who he was, they were terrified. But he forgave and helped them. Later, when their father died, the older brothers were still afraid Joseph might turn against them. He said, "Do not be afraid. Am I in the place of God? You planned to do a bad thing to me. But God planned it for good. . .that many people should be kept alive" (Genesis 50:19–20).

God knows that revenge just messes people up. When you want to get back at someone, *don't*. Let God take care of people and situations in His perfect time.

BIBLE ADVENTURE PRAYER STARTER

Lord, give me patience with
people and trust in You.

BIBLE ADVENTURE MEMORY VERSE

*The Holy Writings say, "I will pay back to
them what they should get, says the Lord."*
ROMANS 12:19

MARY, MOTHER OF JESUS:
KNOW WHERE TO FIND HELP

His mother said to the helpers,
"Do whatever He says."
JOHN 2:5

~~~~~~

If you invited some friends for a sleepover and ran out of your favorite snacks, that would be a bummer. If you set up a much bigger event—say, a wedding dinner—and ran out of something, it would be a disaster.

That's exactly what happened to a man in Bible times. In a village called Cana, not far from Jesus' hometown of Nazareth, a wedding celebration was underway. The man who'd set things up learned there was bad news: the drinks had run out!

The good news is that Mary was there with Jesus. They were invited guests, and when Mary realized what was happening, she asked Jesus to help. Then Mary told the kitchen workers, "Do whatever He says."

Mary knew where to turn for help. Her son—the Son of God—could do anything. And Jesus performed His very first miracle. He told the wedding workers to fill six large pots with water. Then He had them dip some out and take it to the man who'd organized the dinner. What the man tasted was no longer water but very good wine!

That was just a tiny example of what Jesus

could do. The biggest, most important thing He ever did was die on a cross to take the punishment for people's sins. And Mary was there to see that awful event.

It must have been unbelievably hard for her. But Mary knew that Jesus had been born to die. By His death, He became the Savior of the world. Anyone who chose to believe in Him—anyone who accepted Him as Lord—would be saved. Their sins would be wiped clean and they would live forever with Him because He didn't stay dead.

On the most important question of life—how to be saved—Mary knew where to find help. And now you do too!

BIBLE ADVENTURE PRAYER STARTER

Lord Jesus, thank You for dying on the cross for people's sins. I want to accept You as Lord of my life, have my sins wiped away, and enjoy eternity with You.

BIBLE ADVENTURE MEMORY VERSE

If anyone does sin, there is One Who will go between him and the Father. He is Jesus Christ, the One Who is right with God.
1 JOHN 2:1

ABRAHAM:
JUST TRUST GOD

When he was about to go into Egypt, Abram said to his wife Sarai, "I know that you are a beautiful woman. When the men of Egypt see you, they will say, 'This is his wife.' And they will kill me, but they will let you live. Say that you are my sister. Then it may go well with me because of you. And because of you they will not kill me."
GENESIS 12:11–13

You've already read about Abraham who was first known as Abram. He obeyed God's command to pack up, leave home, and go to a place he'd never been before. God promised to make Abraham great, turning his family into an important nation that would bless the whole world. Abraham didn't know it then, but we do now: the blessing would be the birth of Jesus Christ, who offers salvation to all people.

God talked directly to Abraham. God gave Abraham very clear instructions. God made amazing promises to Abraham. You would think Abraham would trust God completely.

You'd be wrong.

Two different times Abraham let fear control him. Both times, it was because of his beautiful wife.

We don't have any pictures of Sarah, who was first known as Sarai. But she must have been a knockout. Twice during his travels, Abraham was afraid the ruler of the country would kill him and steal Sarah. Men love pretty women, and powerful men often do what they can to get what they want. Abraham thought he needed to protect himself, so he asked Sarah to lie and say she was his sister—not his wife.

Sarah joined Abraham in his lies, which were found out each time. The rulers were angry, and Abraham looked bad. Some people might have thought God was fake because Abraham was so dishonest.

He should have just trusted God. If Abraham was supposed to lead a great nation, would God let him die in a squabble over his wife? No!

Abraham is an example for us. Never let people frighten you when you have God on your side. Don't let the fear of others lead you into sin.

BIBLE ADVENTURE PRAYER STARTER

Heavenly Father, give me the courage to trust You and always be truthful.

BIBLE ADVENTURE MEMORY VERSE

The fear of man brings a trap, but he who trusts in the Lord will be honored.
PROVERBS 29:25

SOLOMON:
DO THINGS THAT LAST

In the fourth year of Solomon's rule over Israel. . .he began to build the house of the Lord.

1 KINGS 6:1

Solomon was impressive. The Bible says he was "wiser than all men" (1 Kings 4:31). He spoke three thousand smart sayings called "proverbs" (yep, the book of Proverbs contains many of them) and wrote more than a thousand songs. Solomon also built the temple, "the house of the Lord," the Israelites' place of worship.

Hundreds of years before Solomon, God told Moses to build the "tabernacle." That was Israel's worship center until the time of David, Solomon's father. The tabernacle was really a big tent. In their early days, the Israelites moved around a lot, so their worship center had to move with them. Once Israel became a strong nation under David, though, the king wanted to build a solid, lasting house for God. David drew up plans for a temple in Jerusalem.

But God said no. As king, David had fought many wars. He was doing what God had told him, but the Lord said He wanted His house to be built by a man of peace. That would be David's son Solomon.

When Solomon became king, he spent seven

years building God's temple—and it was beautiful. It was made of stone cut and shaped at a quarry, then put together in Jerusalem without the sound of any hammering. Inside were rich cedar wood walls. There were carvings all around and huge statues of angels, and almost everything was covered in pure gold!

Solomon did things to last. The Israelites used his temple for hundreds of years. And think about this: many of his proverbs and songs are still in our Bibles almost three thousand years later.

We may not be builders or poets like Solomon, but we can also do things that last. Maybe you're making a new friend, setting an example for a younger kid, or helping with vacation Bible school. Whatever you do, do it well. Give your work to God for His glory. It will last all the way into eternity!

BIBLE ADVENTURE PRAYER STARTER

Heavenly Father, I want to do things that last. Help me to honor You with my very best work.

BIBLE ADVENTURE MEMORY VERSE

Your life is set apart for God-like living. The end is life that lasts forever.
ROMANS 6:22

JONATHAN:
TRUE FRIENDSHIP

Jonathan spoke well of David to Saul his father, saying, "Do not let the king sin against his servant David. He has not sinned against you. What he has done has been good for you."
1 Samuel 19:4

Sometimes you meet a person you like right away. You might have the same personality or interests. You might love that person's intelligence, kindness, or sense of humor. When the other person feels the same way about you, a true friendship is born.

An incredible friendship grew up between David—who had just killed Goliath—and Jonathan, the son of Israel's King Saul. Jonathan was a powerful warrior in Israel, and he was next in line to become king. When he met the shepherd-boy-turned-giant-killer, "the soul of Jonathan became one with the soul of David" (1 Samuel 18:1).

But their friendship made Jonathan's dad angry. Saul hated how people sang about David's victory over Goliath. And when Saul realized that Jonathan supported David as the next king, he was furious. "You son of a sinful woman!" he shouted. "Do I not know that you are choosing the son of Jesse to your own shame?" (1 Samuel 20:30).

What a terrible way for a dad to talk to his son. But Jonathan still tried to honor his father while supporting his friend. He had promised before God that he would do anything to help David—and he stuck to that promise. You can see how Jonathan stood up for David in today's Bible verse. That time Saul agreed with Jonathan. But before long, Saul was trying to *kill* both young men. Jonathan warned David and helped him escape.

Jonathan still served his father, and they died together in a battle against the Philistines. David was heartbroken and wrote a song of sorrow for his loyal friend.

We all hope to find a friendship as strong as Jonathan and David's. But even if we don't, we know we have a loyal and loving friend in Jesus— who gave up His life for us. Like Jonathan did with David, let's make a heartfelt commitment to love and honor Jesus in every way.

BIBLE ADVENTURE PRAYER STARTER

Lord Jesus, You gave Yourself for me. May I give my life back to You. Strengthen me to honor and obey You every day.

BIBLE ADVENTURE MEMORY VERSE

A friend loves at all times.
PROVERBS 17:17

JAMES, BROTHER OF JOHN:
THUNDER BROTHER

James and John were brothers. They were the sons of Zebedee. [Jesus] named them Boanerges, which means, The Sons of Thunder.
MARK 3:17

~~~~~~~~~~~

Nicknames often tell you something about people. If you hear of a "Lefty" or a "Ginger" or a "Tank," you'll get a quick idea of that person. Many times that idea is correct.

Jesus once nicknamed James and John, brothers who became His disciples. These sons of a man named Zebedee became the "Sons of Thunder"!

Maybe the nickname meant the guys' dad was wild and loud. Or maybe Jesus was thinking of James and John themselves. There were a couple of times when *they* blew in like a storm. More on that in a moment.

We know quite a bit about John, since he became Jesus' best friend. But the Bible doesn't say nearly as much about James. He's almost always mentioned before John, so he was probably the older of the two. They were working as fishermen when Jesus called them to follow Him. Along with John and Peter, James became part of Jesus' "inner circle," His closest friends among the twelve disciples.

Now, about that "Sons of Thunder" thing. . .

One time, when the people of a Samaritan town disrespected Jesus, James and John wanted to call down fire from heaven to punish them! Another time James and his brother (along with their mom) went to Jesus to ask for the most important spots in heaven—they wanted to sit on thrones on either side of Jesus. When the other disciples learned about that, they weren't too happy with those Sons of Thunder.

But Jesus still loved the two brothers, and they stayed faithful to their Lord. In fact, James became the first of the twelve disciples to be martyred—killed for following Jesus. James had once thundered at Jesus' enemies. In the end, his life thundered love. . .for God and for people.

Think you could be a Thunder Brother (or Sister) today?

BIBLE ADVENTURE PRAYER STARTER

Lord God, sometimes I think and say things I shouldn't. But I know You love me anyway, for Jesus' sake. Please help me to thunder out Your love for all to hear!

BIBLE ADVENTURE MEMORY VERSE

We know what love is because Christ gave His life for us. We should give our lives for our brothers.
1 John 3:16

BEZALEL:
GUTZON BORGLUM

Then Moses said to the people of Israel, "See, the Lord has called by name Bezalel the son of Uri, the son of Hur, of the family of Judah. The Lord has filled him with the Spirit of God, in wisdom, understanding, much learning, and in all work. So he can make plans for working in gold, silver and brass, and cut stones to be set, cut wood, and do good work of every kind."
EXODUS 35:30–33

~~~~~~~~~~

What's a *Gutzon Borglum*? Actually, the question isn't *what* but *who*.

Gutzon Borglum is the guy who made giant carvings of four United States presidents—George Washington, Thomas Jefferson, Abraham Lincoln, and Theodore Roosevelt—on a South Dakota mountainside. His fourteen-year project ended in 1941, the year Borglum died. Eight decades later, more than two million people a year visit Mount Rushmore to see his work.

So what does that have to do with Bible adventures?

Well, not every adventure is about fighting a giant or causing a sea to divide in two. Some adventures are *creative*—like when we use our God-given talents to make books or songs or paintings or other works of art.

Way back in the Old Testament, God chose a man named Bezalel to build the Israelites' tabernacle. That special tent was the people's worship center. One thing Bezalel made for it was a brass altar used in making sacrifices to God. Hundreds of years later, long after Bezalel died, that altar was still around. When Solomon became king, he put the altar in the new worship center—the temple—that he built for God.

Even today, more than three thousand years later, we remember Bezalel for his artistic skill. His talents were God-given, but Bezalel had to put them to work. What talents do you have? Today, how could you use them to honor God and help others?

BIBLE ADVENTURE PRAYER STARTER

Lord, I know You enjoy beautiful things—
because You made mountains and horses
and sunsets and leaves in the autumn!
Thank You for all the beauty I see
around me. Please use me to create more
beauty so that I might honor You.

BIBLE ADVENTURE MEMORY VERSE

So if you eat or drink or whatever
you do, do everything to honor God.
1 CORINTHIANS 10:31

ABIGAIL:
HEADING OFF DISASTER

When Abigail saw David, she got off her donkey in a hurry. Then she put her face to the ground in front of David. She fell at his feet and said, "Let the sin be on me alone, my lord. I beg you,
let your woman servant speak to you."
1 SAMUEL 25:23–24

~~~~~~~~~~~~~~~~~~~

Abigail was a smart, beautiful woman married to a real stinker of a man. Her husband, Nabal, was foolish. His name even means "fool"!

Nabal was wealthy, with thousands of sheep. It was shearing season, when the wool is cut off the animals. They're happy days, because the owner is about to make money from the wool.

Israel's future king, David, was nearby, running for his life from King Saul. David had a band of soldiers who supported him. They'd all been hiding in the desert and needed food and drink. David thought Nabal would be generous at shearing time, so he sent men to ask him for supplies.

"Who is David?" Nabal snorted, insulting him. When David heard, he was furious—and told four hundred men to strap on their swords. He was going to kill Nabal and everyone who worked for him!

When Abigail realized what her foolish husband

had done, she jumped into action. She gathered together two hundred loaves of bread and just as many fig cakes, a hundred bunches of raisins, five roasted sheep, and bottles of wine and rushed them to David. Then she bowed down and apologized for Nabal's behavior. And she urged David not to get himself in trouble by killing people.

David suddenly realized how foolish *he'd* been. And he said, "Thanks be to the Lord God of Israel, Who sent you this day to meet me. May thanks be given for your wisdom. . . . You have kept me this day from being guilty of blood" (1 Samuel 25:32–33).

Almost every day we'll have opportunities to remind people to avoid wrong and to do what's right. Let's be like Abigail and help them head off disaster.

BIBLE ADVENTURE PRAYER STARTER

Father God, help me to speak up when I see a friend making poor choices.

BIBLE ADVENTURE MEMORY VERSE

That person should know that if he turns a sinner from the wrong way, he will save the sinner's soul from death and many sins will be forgiven.
JAMES 5:20

SAUL:
ADVENTURE U-TURN

Saul was still talking much about how he would like to kill the followers of the Lord. He went to the head religious leader. He asked for letters to be written to the Jewish places of worship in the city of Damascus. The letters were to say that if he found any men or women following the Way of Christ he might bring them to Jerusalem in chains.

ACTS 9:1–2

Earlier in this book you read about Saul. Well, you read mostly about *Paul*, which was Saul's new name as a Christian. You saw that he wrote much of the New Testament. You saw that he faced many dangers serving Jesus. You learned that he even got a preview of heaven. Cool, huh?

But do you remember that this great Christian missionary once *hated* Jesus—and everyone who followed Him?

Saul grew up in the city of Tarsus. He was carefully trained in the Jewish scriptures—what we call the Old Testament. Since that part of the Bible says "the Lord our God is one Lord" (Deuteronomy 6:4), Saul didn't believe in Jesus. He couldn't imagine that God had a Son, or that the Son was actually God too. (That's the part of "Trinity" idea you read about earlier.)

Saul wanted to destroy Jesus' followers. But as he went to Damascus to arrest them, he got arrested himself—by Jesus!

The Lord knocked Saul down with a blinding light and said, "Why are you working so hard against Me?" (Acts 9:4). Stunned, Saul asked, "Who are You, Lord?" "I am Jesus," He replied, "the One Whom you are working against" (verse 5). Then Jesus told Saul to go into Damascus for instructions.

Saul suddenly realized that Jesus was real—and he obeyed immediately. Soon Saul was telling everyone about Jesus and how to be saved. He gave up everything for Jesus, risking his life to build the Christian church.

This man thought his adventure would be fighting Jesus. But God turned Saul around, and his life—and the whole world—changed forever. As Paul he would share Jesus with anyone, anywhere, anytime. So should we!

BIBLE ADVENTURE PRAYER STARTER

Lord, thank You for turning Saul around—
and for turning me around too!

BIBLE ADVENTURE MEMORY VERSE

God took us out of a life of darkness.
He has put us in the holy nation
of His much-loved Son.

COLOSSIANS 1:13

JOB:
THE INVISIBLE BATTLEFIELD

There was a man in the land of Uz whose name was Job. That man was without blame. He was right and good, he feared God, and turned away from sin.

JOB 1:1

~~~~~~

Job was on a battlefield but he didn't know it.

He was a very good man. God said, "There is no one like him on the earth. He is without blame, a man who is right and good" (Job 1:8). So why did Job's life suddenly explode like a bomb?

Job was so good that God let Satan test him. What a test it was! Job had no idea why enemy raiders wiped out his servants and flocks of animals. Job couldn't imagine why a tornado knocked down a house and killed his ten children. And Job didn't realize why he got so sick with sores. All those troubles came from Satan, who wanted Job to turn against God.

But the Lord knew Job would stay faithful. He let Job go through tragedies as an example for us, thousands of years later. Job didn't understand what was happening. He got frustrated and angry. But he stuck with God no matter what.

When things go bad in our lives, we might feel like Job—confused, frustrated, and angry. But his story teaches two important truths. First, God limits the trouble Satan can cause. When the devil wanted to attack Job, the Lord said, "All that he has is in your power. Only do not put your hand on him" (Job 1:12). Later, God allowed Satan to attack Job's body but commanded, "Do not kill him" (Job 2:6).

The other lesson comes from the end of Job's story. After struggling so long with his own sickness and loss, Job finally heard from God. He never said exactly why He let Job suffer. But the Lord proved that He knows everything—and that everything that happens in our lives is under His control. God allows good times and bad times for His own wise reasons.

We're all on an invisible battlefield. But our invisible God is always fighting for us.

BIBLE ADVENTURE PRAYER STARTER

Lord, help me to trust You when hard times come. Everything is under Your control!

BIBLE ADVENTURE MEMORY VERSE

Our fight is not with people. It is against the leaders and the powers and the spirits of darkness in this world.
EPHESIANS 6:12

JOHN THE BAPTIST:
KNOW GOD'S WORD

John called two of his followers and sent them to Jesus to ask, "Are You the One Who is to come? Or are we to look for another?" The men came to Jesus and said, "John the Baptist sent us to ask You, 'Are You the One Who is to come? Or are we to look for another?'"
. . . Jesus said to John's followers, "Go back to John the Baptist and tell him what you have seen and heard. Tell him the blind are made to see. Those who could not walk, are walking. Those with a bad skin disease are healed. Those who could not hear, are hearing. The dead are raised to life and poor people have the Good News preached to them."
LUKE 7:19–20, 22

We expect to be punished when we do wrong. But sometimes we find trouble by doing right.

John the Baptist once saw King Herod sinning, so he spoke out boldly. The Bible says, "Herod added another sin by putting John in prison" (Luke 3:20).

We don't know how long John was locked up. But at some point, he started to wonder: Was his relative and friend Jesus really the Messiah, God's special gift to the world? Or should John look for someone else?

John's friends asked Jesus, who gave the answer above. What Jesus said was a summary of things the prophet Isaiah had written around seven hundred years earlier. Isaiah's "messianic prophecies" explained what the Messiah would do when He came. John probably realized that Isaiah's writing described Jesus perfectly.

John the Baptist's life adventure wasn't going exactly as he might have wanted. But John could trust that he was all right. His job was to prepare the way for the Messiah. And Jesus was the Messiah! Everything—even the hard stuff—gets clearer when we know God's Word.

BIBLE ADVENTURE PRAYER STARTER

Heavenly Father, I thank You for giving us Your Word. Please help me to read and understand it. May it change my attitudes and my choices, and make me the person You want me to be.

BIBLE ADVENTURE MEMORY VERSE

"This book of the Law must not leave your mouth. Think about it day and night, so you may be careful to do all that is written in it. Then all will go well with you."

JOSHUA 1:8

BARTIMAEUS:
ADVENTURES IN ASKING

A blind man was sitting by the road. He was asking people for food or money as they passed by. His name was Bartimaeus, the son of Timaeus. He heard that Jesus of Nazareth was passing by. He began to speak with a loud voice, saying, "Jesus, Son of David, take pity on me!"
MARK 10:46–47

〜〜〜〜〜〜〜

Praying is simply talking to God. When we pray, we can praise God—that means we tell Him how great He is. We can thank God for the good things He gives us or does for us. We can confess our sins—tell Him what we've done wrong—and ask for His forgiveness. And we can ask God to help us or other people we know. This last kind of prayer is called a "petition."

Bartimaeus showed how to make petitions to God. He prayed eagerly and clearly until he got an answer.

A blind man in Jericho, Bartimaeus begged for a living. There just weren't many jobs for people without sight. So Bartimaeus sat by the roadside, calling out for others to give him money or food.

His ears worked fine, and he'd been hearing people discuss a miracle worker called Jesus. Then one day Bartimaeus heard people saying Jesus was in town. The blind man started shouting, "Jesus, Son of David, take pity on me!"

Bartimaeus was so loud that other people told him to quiet down. But he kept shouting and shouting until he got Jesus' attention. When Jesus asked what Bartimaeus wanted, he immediately answered, "Lord, I want to see!" (Mark 10:51).

Jesus saw the faith of Bartimaeus and kindly healed his eyes. Now that he could see, Bartimaeus jumped up and followed Jesus down the road.

When you pray, be like Bartimaeus. Don't just say, "Dear God, please bless everyone." Eagerly and clearly ask God for specific things. Then keep asking until He answers. If you are asking for things in His will, He'll do the good things you ask. You'll find that prayer can be an adventure!

BIBLE ADVENTURE PRAYER STARTER

Dear God, please give me boldness to ask You for specific, important things.

BIBLE ADVENTURE MEMORY VERSE

"You are bad and you know how to give good things to your children. How much more will your Father in heaven give good things to those who ask Him?"
MATTHEW 7:11

SARAH:
A DREAM FULFILLED

The Lord said, "I will be sure to return to you at this time next year. And your wife Sarah will have a son."
GENESIS 18:10

~~~~~~~~~~

What do you dream about? Not the nighttime kind of dreams—which are just weird sometimes—but what do you hope to do and be when you get older?

In Bible times, most women dreamed of becoming a mom. Sarah wanted children, but she had never been able to get pregnant. She and her husband, Abraham, were getting older and older. There was no way they could ever have a family.

Well, no *human* way. But nothing is impossible with God.

The Lord had told Abraham that he would become the father of a great nation. But first Abraham had to become the father of *one child*. That was taking years and years to happen. Now he was almost a hundred, and Sarah was almost ninety. It seemed like God's promise was untrue, or that He'd forgotten about it. But God can't be false or forgetful. Sometimes He just has a different schedule than we do.

One day three men walked up to Abraham's tent. One of them was actually God, probably Jesus appearing in a human body long before He was born as a baby in Jerusalem. Abraham quickly invited them to stay for a meal of meat, bread, and cheese.

After the men ate, the Lord said, "I will be sure to return to you at this time next year. And your wife Sarah will have a son." Sarah was inside the tent listening. She chuckled at the thought of a ninety-year-old woman having a baby. Wouldn't you?

But the visitor said, "Is anything too hard for the Lord?" (Genesis 18:14). The answer is, "No!" Sure enough, Sarah had baby Isaac within a year's time.

The adventure of motherhood was long in coming to Sarah. Maybe some of your dreams will take a long time too. But that's okay—if God gave you the dream, He will fulfill it when the time is right. Until then, your job is to stay faithful to Him.

BIBLE ADVENTURE PRAYER STARTER

Heavenly Father, please give me Your dreams—and the patience to wait for Your fulfillment.

BIBLE ADVENTURE MEMORY VERSE

The One Who called you is faithful and will do what He promised.
1 THESSALONIANS 5:24

MORDECAI:
BEFORE ALL THE EXCITEMENT

He had brought up Hadassah, that is Esther, the daughter of his father's brother. For she did not have a father or mother. The young lady was beautiful in body and face. When her father and mother died, Mordecai took her as his own daughter.

ESTHER 2:7

~~~~~~~

Do you have any cousins around your age? They can be so much fun to play with when you're young, and just to hang around with as you grow up.

But some people's cousins are a lot older. That was the case with Esther of the Bible. When her parents died, her cousin Mordecai stepped in to become a dad to her. She lived an adventurous life and became a hero to the Jewish people. But before all the excitement, there was Mordecai.

He was a Jewish man from the Israelite tribe of Benjamin—the same family that produced Israel's first king, Saul. Mordecai had lived in or near Jerusalem until the army of Babylon invaded. He and many other Jews were carried off to Babylon by the enemy king, Nebuchadnezzar.

Now Nebuchadnezzar was dead and Babylon was part of the Persian Empire. Many Jews were living in the capital city of Susa, where Mordecai was raising Esther. When the Persian king, Ahasuerus, got angry with his queen and kicked her out of the palace, he decided to hold a nationwide beauty contest to find a replacement. That's how the beautiful young Esther became queen of Persia—and why she was in place to help save her people, the Jews, from a hateful Persian official named Haman.

Before any of that happened, Mordecai stepped up to help someone in need. That's something all of us can do! If you see a lonely kid at school or know someone in your neighborhood who could use a friend, step up. You never know what a little kindness could accomplish down the road.

BIBLE ADVENTURE PRAYER STARTER

Heavenly Father, please show me ways to help people. If they're lonely, give me the courage to be a friend. If they're weak, use my strength to help them do what needs to be done. I'd like to be as good and helpful as Mordecai!

BIBLE ADVENTURE MEMORY VERSE

Remember to do good and help each other. Gifts like this please God.
HEBREWS 13:16

THOMAS:
WILLING TO DIE WITH JESUS?

*Jesus said to them, "Lazarus is dead. . . .
Come, let us go to him." Thomas, who was
called the Twin, said to the other followers,
"Let us go also so we may die with Jesus."*
JOHN 11:14–16

~~~~~~~~~~~~~~~~~~~~~

If you've ever heard of "Doubting Thomas," he was the apostle in the above scripture. He was one of the twelve guys Jesus chose as followers. Thomas got the "doubting" nickname after Jesus died on the cross and came back to life. Others told Thomas the good news, but he wouldn't believe unless he *saw* Jesus alive. When he did, Thomas said, "My Lord and my God!" (John 20:28).

Sometimes we criticize Thomas for his doubt. But all the disciples made mistakes. In fact, the night Jesus was arrested, "all the followers left Him and ran away" (Matthew 26:56).

A few months earlier, though, Thomas did something brave and good. He urged the other disciples to follow Jesus into danger—even if it killed them!

Jesus' close friend Lazarus was dying. He was from Bethany, a town very close to Jerusalem. Jesus had left Jerusalem just a few days earlier because some people there wanted to kill Him. Now, knowing that Lazarus needed Him, Jesus was going back, close to where His enemies planned to stone Him to death.

Jesus asked the disciples to come along. They must have wondered if Jesus would be killed—and them along with Him. Then Thomas spoke up: "Let us go also so we may die with Jesus."

Nobody knows exactly how Thomas felt right then. Maybe he was eager to face death for his friend Jesus. Or maybe he was really scared. The important thing is that *he went*.

At times we're all afraid of something. But it's important to push forward and do the right thing anyway. Ask God for the strength you need. And know that Jesus is always with you. With Him at your side, you don't need to fear!

BIBLE ADVENTURE PRAYER STARTER

Lord Jesus, I want to be brave even when the adventure of life turns scary. Give me courage to do right since I know You're always with me.

BIBLE ADVENTURE MEMORY VERSE

Do not be afraid of those who hate you. Their hate for you proves they will be destroyed. It proves you have life from God that lasts forever.
PHILIPPIANS 1:28

PHILIP:
ASK THE QUESTION

Philip ran up to him. He saw that the man from Ethiopia was reading from the writings of the early preacher Isaiah and said, "Do you understand what you are reading?"
ACTS 8:30

~~~~~~~

Do you know any kids with the same first name? Maybe there's more than one Liam, Emma, Mason, or Sophia in your group—that's why we have last names. Then you can tell the difference between Mason Lee and Mason Miller or Sophia Jones and Sophia Cruz.

Bible people didn't have last names like ours. But sometimes we use descriptions to tell them apart—like Philip the apostle and Philip the evangelist. Philip the apostle was one of Jesus' original twelve disciples who later became sent-out teachers. Philip the evangelist was a leader in the early church, which began soon after Jesus went up to heaven.

An evangelist preaches good news about Jesus. *Evangel* is another way to say *gospel*, meaning "good news." And Philip was happy to share it wherever he went. . .even though persecution had chased him from his home.

Remember how Saul tried to hurt Christians in the new church in Jerusalem? Most of Jesus' followers ran from the city to protect themselves. Philip went north and preached in a city of Samaria. Then one day an angel told him to go south, into the desert. There was one person there who needed to learn about Jesus!

A man from northern Africa had traveled in a chariot to Jerusalem. He wanted to worship God, but he didn't know Jesus. The man was reading a scroll of the prophet Isaiah. Philip hurried up to his chariot and asked a question: "Do you understand what you are reading?"

The man didn't understand and asked for help. Philip quickly explained that Isaiah's words were all about Jesus. Before long, the man believed in Jesus and was baptized. Then he went back home to Africa and probably told many other people the good news.

Good things happened when Philip asked a question. Let's do the same thing, starting conversations that share the good news of Jesus.

BIBLE ADVENTURE PRAYER STARTER

Lord Jesus, anyone can ask a question. Help me to talk with others about Your gift of salvation.

BIBLE ADVENTURE MEMORY VERSE

Those who lead many to do what is right and good will shine like the stars forever and ever.
DANIEL 12:3

EPAPHRODITUS:
RISKING YOUR LIFE

I thought it was right that I send Epaphroditus back to you. You helped me by sending him to me. We have worked together like brothers. He was like a soldier fighting beside me. He has been wanting to see all of you and was troubled because you heard he was sick. It is true, he was sick. . . . He came close to death while working for Christ. He almost died doing things for me that you could not do.
PHILIPPIANS 2:25–27, 30

~~~~~~~~~~~~~~~~

Bible names are pretty popular these days. You probably know a Caleb or a Hannah or a Daniel or a Rachel. Maybe one of those is your own name!

But have you ever met a kid named *Epaphroditus*? It's not common today, but it was apparently popular enough in the apostle Paul's time. And Paul was grateful for the help of a man by that name.

Mr. E did something adventurous—he risked his life to help Paul's ministry. Christians in the city of Philippi decided to send Paul some kind of gift (Philippians 4:18). Perhaps it was money; maybe it was food and clothing. Epaphroditus delivered the gift, but while he was with Paul, he got really sick—so sick that he almost died. Paul didn't say exactly what happened to Epaphroditus, but we can guess that he might have drunk some bad water or been bitten by a mosquito that was carrying a disease. (Those things can happen to missionaries around the world even today.)

Happily, for Epaphroditus, God healed him. Then the man with the long, funny name continued "like a soldier fighting beside" Paul.

We should always be willing to help with God's work, even if it costs us. We probably won't risk our lives, but even if we do, God has us covered—by the eternal life Jesus gives!

BIBLE ADVENTURE PRAYER STARTER

Lord Jesus, You gave Your life on the cross for me. Please help me to offer my everything back to You.

BIBLE ADVENTURE MEMORY VERSE

Those who plant with tears will gather fruit with songs of joy.
PSALM 126:5

DORCAS:
ADVENTURES IN KINDNESS

All the women whose husbands had died were standing around crying. They were showing the clothes Dorcas had made while she was with them.

ACTS 9:39

~~~~~~~~~~~~

At some point in life, everyone starts to think about dying. Many people plan for how they want to be remembered. Some work hard to build a business with their name on it. Others try to get elected to political office or write an important book or set records in a sport. But how about being remembered for your kindness?

Not many years after Jesus died, rose again, and returned to heaven, His followers were spreading the good news all around. In a place called Joppa, a city on the coast of the Mediterranean Sea, there was a Christian woman named Dorcas. According to Luke, who wrote the book of Acts, "she did many good things and many acts of kindness" (Acts 9:36).

Dorcas had a heart for widows—women whose husbands had died. She sewed clothes for them, which was a big help since widows were often very poor. When Dorcas got sick and died, the widows were heartbroken. Someone called the apostle Peter to come to Joppa. When he arrived, the crying widows told him all the nice things Dorcas had done for them.

What a great way to be remembered! Everyone Dorcas had helped spoke well of her, and God even told her story in His Word. We're still talking about Dorcas two thousand years after she died.

But Dorcas is remembered for more than just her kindness. Peter, the leader of Jesus' disciples and one of the most important people in the early church, prayed that God would bring Dorcas back to life. . .and God did! Peter took her by the hand and brought her back to the widows, who then cried tears of joy.

God doesn't save us because we're kind—but after He saves us, He wants us to be kind. Dorcas is remembered today for her kindness. Why not aim for that yourself?

BIBLE ADVENTURE PRAYER STARTER

Lord Jesus, Dorcas was kind to people in need, just like You were. I want to be that way too—may I be remembered for sharing Your goodness.

BIBLE ADVENTURE MEMORY VERSE

The fruit that comes from having the Holy Spirit in our lives is: love, joy, peace, not giving up, being kind.
GALATIANS 5:22

MARK:
DON'T GO IT ALONE

I have known Silvanus as a faithful Christian brother and it is by him I have written this short letter to help you. It tells you of the true loving-favor of God. Stay true in His loving-favor. The church which is in the city of Babylon says hello. It has been chosen by God the same as you have been. My son, Mark, says hello also.

1 PETER 5:12–13

Why does your Bible have a "book of Mark"?

We know that the apostle Paul was upset when Mark ran away from a mission trip (Acts 15). Earlier, Mark may also have run away when Jesus was arrested. Mark 14:51–52 describes a young man "following Him with only a piece of cloth around his body. They put their hands on the young man. Leaving the cloth behind, he ran away with no clothes on." Many people think that Mark, years after Jesus' death on the cross, wrote that embarrassing story about himself.

Over time, though, something really changed for this young man. He became a great help to Paul (2 Timothy 4:11) and a "son" to the apostle Peter (1 Peter 5:13). It seems that Mark worked with Peter, learning from him and collecting details he would later write down in the second of the four Gospels—Matthew, Mark, Luke, and John.

Mark found in Peter a *mentor*—an older, wiser person who helped him learn and grow. For many of us, our parents are our greatest mentors. Sometimes it may be an uncle or an aunt or a grandparent. Maybe it's a Sunday school teacher or a coach or a neighbor. Whoever that person is, be willing to listen and learn. God puts older believers into our lives to make us better. . .to help us become more like Jesus.

BIBLE ADVENTURE PRAYER STARTER

Lord Jesus, I want to be more like You. Please give me a mentor who sets a great example. I want to learn from and be like those older people who have lived their lives for Your glory.

BIBLE ADVENTURE MEMORY VERSE

Christian brothers, live your lives as I have lived mine. Watch those who live as I have taught you to live.
PHILIPPIANS 3:17

BENAIAH:
WHAT'S BETTER THAN TOUGHNESS?

Benaiah the son of Jehoiada, the son of a powerful soldier from Kabzeel, did great things. . . . He killed an Egyptian who was very tall, five cubits tall. The Egyptian held a spear as big as the cross-piece of a cloth-maker. But Benaiah went down to him with a heavy stick and took the spear from the Egyptian's hand. Then he killed him with his own spear.

1 CHRONICLES 11:22–23

You don't find many people more adventurous than Benaiah. He was a professional soldier in King David's army. Benaiah did amazing things on the battlefield, as the scripture above proves. Another time, on a snowy day, he even fought with a lion in a pit! (Spoiler alert: Benaiah came out as the winner.)

He was one of Israel's thirty top soldiers—out of almost three hundred thousand men. He commanded twenty-four thousand other soldiers all by himself.

But Benaiah was more than toughness. He was also completely loyal to David, God's choice for king in Israel. David chose Benaiah to lead the soldiers of his own bodyguard. And years later, when David was old and one of David's sons tried to steal the throne, Benaiah made sure the right son—Solomon—was crowned instead.

Very few of us will ever be as strong as Benaiah. Not many of us will ever be as brave. But every one of us can be loyal—to our family, to our friends, and to God. With His help, we can stand up for Him and the people we love.

This world can be a tough and scary place. Sometimes other Christians will need your support. Choose to love, honor, and help them like Benaiah did for David. Loyalty is a powerful thing—even better than toughness.

BIBLE ADVENTURE PRAYER STARTER

Lord God, please make me strong to stand up for You, my family, and my friends. I want to be loyal to You when other people laugh. I want to defend my loved ones when they're under attack. I want to be a modern Benaiah!

BIBLE ADVENTURE MEMORY VERSE

Dear friends, let us love each other, because love comes from God. Those who love are God's children and they know God.
1 John 4:7

PETER:
THE COMEBACK

Peter said to them, "Be sorry for your sins and turn from them and be baptized in the name of Jesus Christ, and your sins will be forgiven."... Those who believed what he said were baptized. There were about 3,000 more followers added that day.

ACTS 2:38, 41

If a football team is behind by 17 points in the second half, the game is pretty much over. If a baseball team gets down by 7 or a soccer team by 3, chances are they're going to lose.

But once in a while a team that's way down will start to get hot. They might even pull out a victory. Fans call that a "comeback."

It was no game for the apostle Peter, but he sure needed a comeback. The leader of Jesus' apostles had really messed up. When Jesus was arrested, Peter got so scared that he said he didn't even know Jesus. That was a terrible thing to do. But then Peter did it again. . .and *again*!

Jesus had said all twelve disciples would leave Him that night. But Peter argued: "Even if all men give up and turn away because of You, I will never" (Matthew 26:33). Jesus knows everything, though, and He said that before the rooster crowed in the morning, Peter would deny Jesus three times. That's exactly what happened.

But Jesus is kind and forgiving. After He died on the cross and came back to life, Jesus found Peter and told him—three times—to take care of other believers. Jesus forgave Peter and gave him a very important job. Peter would help build Jesus' church on earth.

He did an excellent job. Not because of his own goodness, but because he let God use him. As you read in today's scripture, Peter preached a sermon that brought thousands of people to Jesus. Now the church has hundreds of millions of members around the world.

Peter had a great comeback after messing up. So can we. Just admit your sins to God, ask for His forgiveness, and get back in the game.

BIBLE ADVENTURE PRAYER STARTER

Lord, please forgive me when I fail You and put me back to work—Your work.

BIBLE ADVENTURE MEMORY VERSE

"Remember how you once loved Me. Be sorry for your sin and love Me again as you did at first."
REVELATION 2:5

ISAAC:
"UM, DAD. . .
WHAT ARE YOU DOING"

Isaac said to Abraham, "My father!" Abraham
answered, "Here I am, my son." Isaac said,
"See, here is the fire and the wood. But
where is the lamb for the burnt gift?"
GENESIS 22:7

~~~~~~~~~~~~

Do you remember the miracle child born to hundred-year-old Abraham? He called the baby *Isaac*, meaning "he laughs." It would be funny to have a kid at that age!

God had promised that Abraham would become a great nation, with as many people as the stars. That sounded great—except Abraham had *zero* kids. God never lies, though, and He said Abraham would have a child with his wife, Sarah, no matter how old they were.

Well, Sarah did have Isaac, and everyone was happy. Then one day. . .

God said to Abraham, "Take now your son, your only son, Isaac, whom you love. And go to the land of Moriah. Give him as a burnt gift on the altar in worship" (Genesis 22:2).

We don't know what Abraham thought. But he obeyed. Abraham got up early, loading a donkey with firewood. Then he and Isaac went to a mountaintop.

There Isaac asked, "Where is the lamb for the burnt gift?" He didn't realize that *he* was the sacrifice!

Abraham answered, "God will have for Himself a lamb ready" (Genesis 22:8). Then the father tied his son with a rope and put him on the altar. Can you imagine Isaac asking, "Um, Dad, what are you doing?"

The Bible doesn't say what Isaac thought. But it seems he didn't argue. Abraham was ready to kill Isaac when God's angel stopped him. "Do nothing to him," the angel said. "Now I know that you fear God. You have not kept from Me your son, your only son" (Genesis 22:12).

Does that phrase "only son" sound familiar? That's how God the Father described Jesus! God the Father *did* sacrifice His only Son so that we could be saved. When we believe and receive Jesus, we gain life that lasts forever.

BIBLE ADVENTURE PRAYER STARTER

Wow, Lord—thank You for the sacrifice of Your only Son. I want the eternal life He offers.

BIBLE ADVENTURE MEMORY VERSE

"For God so loved the world that He gave His only Son. Whoever puts his trust in God's Son will not be lost but will have life that lasts forever."
JOHN 3:16

HANNAH:
PRAY HARD

Hannah was very troubled. She prayed to the Lord and cried with sorrow. Then she made a promise and said, "O Lord of All, be sure to look on the trouble of Your woman servant, and remember me. Do not forget Your woman servant, but give me a son. If You will, then I will give him to the Lord all his life."
1 SAMUEL 1:10–11

Ever think about being a parent? At your age, maybe a few boys have. Lots of girls dream of being a mom.

In the Bible, Hannah longed for a child. She was old enough to be a mom, but she couldn't get pregnant. That was tough. Her husband made things even worse by marrying another woman. In the old days, some men did that—and it never went well.

The other woman did have kids—and she made fun of Hannah. Hannah was so sad she could hardly eat.

But Hannah was wise. She took her problem to God in prayer. At the place of worship, she poured out her heart. Hannah asked God specifically for a son. Then she promised to give him back so he could serve God his whole life.

Hannah prayed so hard that the priest Eli thought she was drunk! She explained that she was just really sad and hopeful. Eli answered, "May the God of Israel do what you have asked of Him" (1 Samuel 1:17).

God did—He gave Hannah a baby. When Samuel was just a boy, Hannah took him back to the tabernacle to help Eli. Samuel grew up to be a great prophet, guiding Israel toward God. That all happened because Hannah prayed—hard.

If we don't ask in God's will, God doesn't give us what we ask. Like any parent, He knows better than we do. So sometimes He says no for our own good. (Think about it: Would your parents give you a stick of dynamite if you asked?) But many times, God will say yes. Either way, like your parents, He loves to hear from you.

So talk to God. Pray hard. And when He gives you what you want, remember to praise Him like Hannah did. (Read her follow-up prayer in 1 Samuel 2:1–10!)

BIBLE ADVENTURE PRAYER STARTER

Lord God, may I ask You for good things and praise You when You answer.

BIBLE ADVENTURE MEMORY VERSE

Never stop praying.
1 THESSALONIANS 5:17

MATTHEW:
STEP INTO NEW LIFE

As Jesus went from there, He saw a man called Matthew. Matthew was sitting at his work gathering taxes. Jesus said to him, "Follow Me." Matthew got up and followed Jesus.

MATTHEW 9:9

~~~~~~~~~

If you remember the story of Zaccheus, you know that tax collectors were not popular people in Jesus' time. But Jesus loved unpopular tax collectors as much as He loved anyone else—enough to die for their sins. Zaccheus was saved and became a follower of Jesus. Same with Matthew.

Jesus was living in a town called Capernaum, near the Sea of Galilee. He had already made disciples of two sets of brothers—Peter and Andrew, and James and John—who made their living fishing on the big lake. Now, walking through town, Jesus saw Matthew doing *his* job: collecting taxes. Jesus said, "Follow Me," and Matthew got up immediately. He walked away from collecting taxes to walk in Jesus' footsteps.

Matthew became a *disciple* of Jesus, one of the twelve men specially chosen to learn about God's plan of salvation. Once they understood that plan, Jesus would send them out as *apostles*, no longer learners but teachers themselves.

One of the first things Matthew did was invite Jesus to dinner. Tax collectors had plenty of money, and Matthew invited a lot of people—his tax collector friends and other unpopular people. The Jewish religious leaders saw the guests and grumbled to the disciples, "Why does your Teacher eat with men who gather taxes and with sinners?" (Matthew 9:11). Jesus responded by saying He hadn't come to earth to save people who thought they were good. He came to save people who knew they were sinners.

Matthew realized that he was a sinner, so when Jesus invited him to a new life, he stepped right up. Have you done the same? To be saved, just admit to God that you have sinned by disobeying Him. Ask Him to save you through your belief in His Son, Jesus. Then you'll enjoy the fresh new life that Matthew did—forever!

BIBLE ADVENTURE PRAYER STARTER

Jesus, You are the only way to God the Father. I believe in You—make me part of God's family!

BIBLE ADVENTURE MEMORY VERSE

"I am the Door. Anyone who goes in through Me will be saved from the punishment of sin."
JOHN 10:9

MOSES:
DON'T MISS THE ADVENTURE

Moses said to the Lord, "Lord, I am not a man of words. . . . I am slow in talking and it is difficult for me to speak." Then the Lord said to him, "Who has made man's mouth? Who makes a man not able to speak or hear? Who makes one blind or able to see? Is it not I, the Lord? So go now. And I will be with your mouth. I will teach you what to say." But Moses said, "O Lord, I ask of You, send some other person."
EXODUS 4:10-13

Moses is a huge Bible hero. But he tried not to be.

From way back, God had special plans for Moses. He was born when God's people lived in Egypt—and the king, called Pharaoh, ordered Israelite babies to be drowned in the Nile River. Moses' mom did put him in the river—in a floating basket. Then Pharaoh's daughter found him and took him home as her own child. So Moses, who should have been dead, grew up in a palace! (Do you think God might have had something to do with that?)

God saved Moses so he could save God's people. He was to lead the Israelites out of their slavery in Egypt. But Moses got nervous. He asked God to send someone else.

That request actually made God angry—but He still wanted Moses to do the job. So God offered to send Moses' older brother, Aaron, along too. Aaron would do the talking while Moses performed the miracles.

That's exactly what happened. And Moses and Aaron led the Israelites out of Egypt, through the Red Sea, and toward their promised land of Canaan.

Sometimes God gives us jobs that seem way too big. We think, *There's no way I could do that!* And that's true—we can't. But God can. So just let Him work *through* you.

BIBLE ADVENTURE PRAYER STARTER

Lord God, sometimes I feel like Moses—that I can't speak up for You. But I know You will give me the words and the courage. Please do that today!

BIBLE ADVENTURE MEMORY VERSE

He answered me, "I am all you need. I give you My loving-favor. My power works best in weak people." I am happy to be weak and have troubles so I can have Christ's power in me.
2 CORINTHIANS 12:9

JEREMIAH:
FAITHFUL, NO MATTER WHAT

They took Jeremiah and put him into the well. . .letting him down with ropes. There was no water in the well, but only mud. And Jeremiah went down into the mud.

JEREMIAH 38:6

~~~~~~~~~~~~~~~~~~~~

Jeremiah's "adventure" wasn't always fun. In fact, his life was really hard. But he stayed faithful to God, no matter what. Jeremiah believed that God had a great future for His people, even if life now was full of trouble and sadness.

Jeremiah was a priest's son living near Jerusalem. When he was quite young—maybe around thirteen—Jeremiah heard directly from God. "Before I started to put you together in your mother, I knew you," the Lord told the boy. "Before you were born, I set you apart as holy. I chose you to speak to the nations for Me" (Jeremiah 1:5).

God wanted Jeremiah to be His prophet, but Jeremiah thought he was too young. "Do not say, 'I am only a boy,' " God responded. "You must go everywhere I send you. And you must say whatever I tell you" (Jeremiah 1:7).

Jeremiah obeyed, preaching God's word to the people of Judah. They were very sinful, so the message was full of warnings. People don't like to be told they're wrong, and they hated Jeremiah's words. They treated him terribly. They argued. They attacked him. They beat him and put him in jail. Once, as you saw above, Jeremiah was dropped down a muddy well as punishment!

For forty long, hard years, Jeremiah tried to get people to obey God. They never did, so the Lord finally sent the Babylonians to punish Jerusalem and Judah. Jeremiah knew trouble was coming, which made him very sad. He was nicknamed the "weeping prophet."

How could Jeremiah stay faithful when life was so hard? Only because he trusted God's goodness. "I have loved you with a love that lasts forever," God told Israel (Jeremiah 31:3). He had good plans that stretched out forever for everyone who obeys Him—people like Jeremiah and people like *you*.

BIBLE ADVENTURE PRAYER STARTER

Lord, my world can be sad and hard like Jeremiah's. Help me to stay faithful, no matter what, and trust in Your good plans.

BIBLE ADVENTURE MEMORY VERSE

" 'I know the plans I have for you,' says the Lord, 'plans for well-being and not for trouble, to give you a future and a hope.' "
JEREMIAH 29:11

LAZARUS:
REFLECTING JESUS' POWER

Jesus had raised Lazarus from the dead. The religious leaders of the Jews talked together about having Lazarus killed also. Because of Lazarus, many Jews were leaving their own religion. They were putting their trust in Jesus.
JOHN 12:9–11

~~~~~~~~~~~~~~~~

The Bible is a serious book. In many ways, it's a matter of life and death—it warns of the punishment for our sin but also tells us how to be saved by believing in Jesus.

Once in a while, though, you'll find something funny in the Bible. Like the verses above. Did you catch what's happening there?

Jesus' friend Lazarus had been sick. The man's sisters, Mary and Martha, sent word to Jesus asking for help. He and His disciples were far away, and Jesus waited two whole days before He left. By the time He arrived in His friends' town of Bethany, Lazarus had been dead—for four days.

Mary and Martha both said, "Lord, if You had been here, my brother would not have died" (John 11:21, 32). They thought Jesus was four days late. But Jesus was right on time—to do something amazing.

He ordered the burial cave to be opened. Jesus prayed and then shouted, "Lazarus, come out!" (John 11:43). Suddenly the dead man was alive! He stumbled out of the tomb, still wrapped in his graveclothes. Jesus told the people to unwrap Lazarus and let him go.

Wouldn't it be amazing to see a dead man alive again? Lots of people did see that, and they told others. Before long, many of those people were following Jesus, the man with the power to give life.

Then the story gets funny. The Jewish religious leaders, who hated Jesus' popularity, decided they should get rid of Lazarus. So they talked about killing the man who'd been dead! Didn't they realize Jesus could just bring him back to life again?

Lazarus reflected Jesus' power. When people saw Lazarus, they knew what Jesus had done for him. Jesus has done great things for us too. Let's reflect His power in our own lives!

BIBLE ADVENTURE PRAYER STARTER

Lord Jesus, when people see me, I want them to think of You. Help me to reflect Your power and goodness in all I do.

BIBLE ADVENTURE MEMORY VERSE

We know that our life in this world is His life lived in us.
1 JOHN 4:17

JESUS:
"I AM COMING SOON!"

"See! I am coming soon. I am bringing with Me the reward I will give to everyone for what he has done."
REVELATION 22:12

Don't you love Bible stories about Jesus? That His birth was told hundreds of years earlier by the prophets. . .that He was born in a Bethlehem stable and got His first visit from shepherds. . .that He grew up to teach and preach and perform miracles like walking on water, healing the sick, and raising the dead. . .that He allowed Himself to be killed on a cross to take the punishment for our sins. . .that He came back to life and then rose up into the sky on His way back to heaven!

All those things really happened. The Bible is a history book telling us the most important stuff. But Jesus' friend John wrote, "There are many other things which Jesus did also. If they were all written down, I do not think the world itself could hold the books that would be written" (John 21:25).

Now, don't think that Jesus' story is all in the past. He's alive and working, right now, in heaven. Jesus once told His disciples, "There are many rooms in My Father's house. . . . I am going away to make a place for you. After I go and make a place for you, I will come back and take You with Me" (John 14:2–3).

As you see in Revelation 22:12, Jesus says He's coming back *soon*. And He's going to fix everything that's wrong with our world. He'll reward all of us who trust and follow Him. He'll punish Satan and his followers. In the end, heaven will come to earth—and Jesus will be King of a perfect new world without any tears or pain or death. Forever!

Every Bible story, every Bible character, really points to Jesus—actually, the whole universe does. But even though He is the all-powerful God who created everything and keeps it running, He knows and loves *you* personally. And He's coming soon to see you!

BIBLE ADVENTURE PRAYER STARTER

Jesus, thanks for everything! I look forward to seeing You face-to-face.

BIBLE ADVENTURE MEMORY VERSE

"You must be ready also. The Son of Man is coming at a time when you do not think He will come."
LUKE 12:40

BIBLE STORY MATCH!

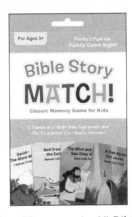

This exciting "2-games-in-1" Bible memory match is inspired by Old Testament and New Testament Bible story favorites. Deck one features cards with art from Old Testament stories, including Noah's Ark, Baby Moses, the Parting of the Red Sea, Strong Man Samson, Jonah and the Whale, and Queen Esther. Deck two includes art from New Testament stories like Jesus Is Born, Fishers of Men, the Woman at the Well, Jesus Walks on Water, the Good Samaritan, the Empty Tomb, and many more!

978-1-64352-279-1 / Boxed Puzzle